D0648040

Necessary Roughness

with Connections

Necessary Roughness

Marie G. Lee

with
Connections

HOLT, RINEHART AND WINSTON

A Harcourt Education Company

Austin • Orlando • Chicago • New York • Toronto • London • San Diego

For permission to reprint copyrighted material, grateful acknowledgment is made to the following sources:

HarperCollins Publishers: *Necessary Roughness* by Marie G. Lee. Copyright © 1996 by Marie G. Lee.

Arte Publico Press: "Refugee Ship" by Lorna Dee Cervantes from *The Americas Review,* 1982. Copyright © 1982 by Lorna Dee Cervantes. Published by Arte Publico Press - University of Houston, 1982.
Dell Publishing, a division of Random House, Inc.: From *Children of the River* by Linda Crew. Copyright © 1989 by Linda Crew.
Los Angeles Times: From "Success Saga in America: Korean Style" by Elizabeth Mehren from *Los Angeles Times,* August 12, 1987. Copyright © 1987 by Los Angeles Times.
Random House Children's Books, a division of Random House, Inc.: "Stealing for Girls" by Will Weaver from *Ultimate Sports* by Donald R. Gallo. Copyright © 1995 by Donald R. Gallo.

Cover Design: Chris Smith; Cover Photography: Sam Dudgeon/HRW Photo

HRW is a trademark licensed to Holt, Rinehart and Winston, registered in the United States of America and/or other jurisdictions.

Printed in the United States of America

ISBN 0-03-067524-3

5 6 7 043 08 07 06

To Michelle "Gi" Lee

acknowledgments

This book took a lot longer than I thought it would. Thank you, thank you, thank you to family and friends who helped me see it through.

Thanks, Mom and Dad, for everything. Thank you, Ginee Seo, for being a wonderful editor and friend; Wendy Schmalz, same, for being my agent. And to Cylin Busby for her insightful comments. Thank you, Sheila Hamanaka, for taking my cat to the "dentist."

Thanks to the Hibbing High School football team (especially Craig Massich) for letting me watch.

Thanks for the literary advice about football to Tom, Dean, Karl, Ken, and especially Paul Choi.

And thanks. You know who you are.

Contents

one

Okay, I shouldn't have done it. They say hindsight is twenty-twenty; my visibility is now unlimited. I shouldn't have even dreamed of saying anything about the Buddha. But what can I say except that, at the time, it seemed a perfectly logical thing to do?

The Buddha statue in question was the size of a Border collie and about three times as heavy. Pure stone, very Las Vegas in gold-leaf paint. It always sat in the left corner of our living room, its smile semi-hidden behind the potted palm.

No one ever paid any attention to it. We didn't offer it food like the Parks did with theirs. It just sat there. So when my mother said we needed to leave things behind for the big move, I suggested that.

Naturally. We say grace before meals, which means we're Christians, which means we have no need for a *Buddha* statue—right? And the Parks certainly would have appreciated the donation, two Buddhas being better than one and all that.

But as usual, after I said it I wished I hadn't. I still don't know exactly why that lump of stone was so important, but Abogee boiled over, as if I'd suggested we leave my sister behind or something. And I knew he was mad, not because he ranted and raved or whopped me on my heinie with a yardstick—like he used to when I was little—but because he refused to talk to me, or even look at me, the whole drive to Minnesota.

When my abogee gets mad, he either yells or gives you the silent treatment, depending on his mood. I almost prefer the yelling because eventually it blows over. It's his silence that really cuts, the way a piece of paper can slice your finger open.

But this time I didn't let him get to me. I was mad too, and we kind of canceled each other out.

I couldn't believe it when Abogee told us we were leaving L.A. I think the first words out of my mouth were "But we can't. I haven't finished high school yet!"

O-Ma (Young and I call her by the Korean word for mom, while Abogee makes us call him Abogee—father) made me go outside, which is rare for her. I didn't stop to think that she was probably upset too. I mean, she was leaving all her friends, her church, and Kim's Green Extravaganza, our store.

I felt even worse when Young didn't complain, even though a week ago she'd found out that—after about a kajillion auditions—she'd won a spot in the L.A. Young (no relation) People's Orchestra.

She just nodded when she heard the news, which made Abogee say to me, "Why can't you be more obedient like your sister?"

It always boils down to this: I'm the evil twin and Young is the good one.

Last night through the wall I heard Abogee tell O-Ma that if we were in Korea, I would never talk back to him like I do. So how does he know? How can he predict what I'd be like?

I would say that we're an almost perfect family, except for the one small fact that Abogee and I could start World War III all by ourselves. The way Abogee talks, you'd think he had me mixed up with some other son. One who gets all A's. One who knows what his abogee wants before he says anything. One who snaps to attention and goes "Yessir!" at everything his abogee says.

And as for me, my life is defined by the perpetual fear of pissing him off. I never mean to, like I said, but it's like walking through a minefield. No matter how much you tiptoe around, sooner or later—*boom!*—you're going to get it.

So there we were, in a clanky station wagon, the Buddha statue weighing down the rear, heading toward Minnesota. Toward certain doom.

two

According to our espionage reports, it was Abogee's brother who got us into this mess. Even though Young and I aren't allowed in on family affairs, we manage to piece things together, especially since the walls that separate the rooms in our house are as thin as rice crackers.

Let me back up to give you a little history. Abogee and O-Ma came to America when Young and I were three. Abogee had been a chemist, so he wasn't too thrilled with O-Ma's idea of opening a grocery—even though his Ph.D. friends Mr. Park and Mr. Lee also had stores. But when he couldn't find a position in chemistry, he went along with O-Ma's idea, grumbling all the way.

O-Ma named our store Kim's Green Extravaganza. We sold all sorts of veggies and fruits and went mental about keeping them extra fresh. The moment something got even a little soft or had one tiny little bruise, we either gave it away to friends or took it home. To this day I'm haunted by the spongy taste of overripe apples.

The other thing about the store was that we sold stuff our customers needed: soup-for-one, tiny cans of cat food, cigarettes, fat-free cookies. O-Ma even went so far as to ask for suggestions. Abogee complained that people would think we didn't know how to run a business. But the stuff O-Ma ordered from people's suggestions almost always became regular sellers.

I guess we were doing pretty well, because Abogee's mom and his brother, Bong, eventually came from Korea to live with us.

At first I wasn't too thrilled to be sharing the house with two strangers, but Grandma, Halmoni, grew on me. She padded around in her stocking feet, and when I came home from school, I could hear her singing wafting through the open windows. Some of my best memories are of sitting with her in the kitchen. Young would be at her flute lessons, so it was just Halmoni and me, surrounded by pungent Korean food smells—ginger, garlic, sesame oil. She would chop, smash, fry, and boil like a maniac while she told me stories about animals: why frogs croak in the rain, how the rat king found the perfect husband for his daughter.

Bong told stories too. They were all about this guy, Joker Kim, who can't stop himself from doing weird and/or stupid things; like he'd pick his nose and then get bummed when a glop of snot fell in his rice. Young and I hated it when he'd call us over and say, "Did you hear the one about when Joker Kim went to the bathroom?"

I always had the feeling Abogee was not thrilled with his brother either. It was clear that Bong cared only about Bong. He never made his bed; he splattered toothpaste all over the bathroom. The closest he ever came to helping with the dishes was one time when he brought his glass within a hundred-yard vicinity of the sink.

At the store he wasn't much better. Once, a whole crate of Clementine oranges disappeared when he was supposed to be watching them. But Abogee just made his regular guy, Manuel, pick up the slack. Abogee let Bong do his thing all the way up until he stopped showing up for work. Then Abogee fired him.

After that, Bong just drifted in and out of the house, sometimes disappearing for days at a time. Occasionally he'd come in with his face looking like a bruised piece of fruit and smelling like he'd been smoked and pickled.

Everything in the house somehow managed to stay its course until Halmoni died. I think Halmoni kept a lid on whatever grudges lurked between

Abogee and Bong. Once she was gone, I could hear them arguing long into the night.

Bong started reading these magazines, *Small Business Owner, Entrepreneur*, that he left behind the toilet in the bathroom. One day he announced that he was now the proud owner of a convenience store somewhere up in Minnesota. The next thing we knew—*poof!*—he was gone, and we had some peace.

Of course, the next thing we knew—*poof!*—Bong turned up in Korea with some scheme about pizza-making robots he'd found through an 800 number. Hello! It was so important, he didn't have time to tell anyone, didn't have time to sell the store back in Minnesota. He promised that one day he'd be rich and pay everyone back.

It was at this point that O-Ma found out that Abogee had loaned Bong a wad of money to buy the store, a franchise. In fact Bong had convinced Abogee to basically stake him all of the money, since he didn't have any of his own. That was when Young and I got the news that we were moving.

Abogee keeps telling us that he's been looking for an excuse to get out of L.A. anyway. It's too crowded, too many merchants getting shot in their stores. The new place is going to be quiet, safe, secure. A small town, good schools. No more big-city problems.

It gets to me, that Abogee even pretends he's

doing this for Young and me. O-Ma is always saying, "Your father sacrifices so much for you. Look at how hard he works at the store. It's all for you children."

If that's true, then he doesn't have to do this. He could sacrifice less and we could stay in L.A. and that would be *fine* with me.

I would have said this out loud, but I knew no one would have listened.

three

Young and I had named our car Lou, because he came to us with a key chain that said LOU GRUBB CHEVROLET FORD, and he seemed more like a Lou than a Grubb. Lou was the latest in a series of junker cars that Abogee had bought cheap, counting on his mechanic friend, Henry Park, to fix things when necessary. That was fine in L.A. But as each minute passed, as we drove farther and farther away from Henry and his tools, I worried that every little noise might be Lou's death rattle.

We were inching up the twisty cliff road that crosses the Continental Divide, when Lou started to sputter and cough. There was no shoulder, only a tinfoil guardrail that could not have kept a mosquito from going over the edge, so Abogee kept going.

As we climbed higher, Lou wheezed louder. The CHECK ENGINE light flickered. O-Ma murmured something to Abogee that I couldn't hear.

Young and I, stuffed in the backseat along with shoe boxes, bags of linens, that damn Buddha, and a cooler, looked at each other and clung to the worn armrests. Abogee shifted Lou into another gear.

The car started to slide backward.

Young grabbed my hand. Rocky crags we'd passed seconds earlier were now passing us. I touched the Buddha's nose.

If we go, you go, I reminded him.

The gear caught. Lou jerked to a stop, then slowly, reluctantly moved forward.

We finally came to one of those places where you can pull over to let people pass if you're going too slow, which we were. Some jerk in a Geo Tracker honked at us, spraying gravel—*ping! ping! ping!*—as he passed, while Abogee struggled to wedge Lou into the tiny pull-off. Young and I got out and inspected the cliff while Abogee fiddled under the hood.

It felt good to be standing on solid ground.

"Did you know that at the Continental Divide, rivers actually change direction?" Young asked.

"Mmm." Fingers of a breeze teased my sweaty hair. I liked this place, the endless chain of mountains, the scrubby trees clinging like undecided suicide jumpers to the edges of cliffs. I yelled "Hel-loooo" into the air, hoping for an echo, but there was none.

Half an hour and two quarts of oil later, we were on our way again. Lou sounded better, but I think it was the rest more than the tinkering that did it. We crested the Divide, then began the equally twisty ride down. I was wondering at exactly what point the rivers flowed in opposite directions, but Young was asleep and I didn't want to bug her.

After we left the mountains behind, the ride flattened out. I almost preferred being in a state of panic. Now I had nothing to do except sit and think about how much I missed my friends, my soccer team, our old hangouts. You don't know what you've got till it's gone.

"You don't know what you've got till it's gone." That's what SuJin had said to me the night before we left. I know it's corny, but for this situation, it's applicable. SuJin was always into prepackaged words. Her other favorite line was, "If you love something, set it free"—and blah-blah-blah. I can't remember the rest. I think she got them off posters in card stores.

SuJin is—was—my girlfriend. She was also Young's best friend, so I didn't have to sneak around to see her. A lot of Korean parents are strict, but not as bad as Abogee. He'd decreed dating totally off-limits until college. Who is he kidding?

Even though I got to *see* SuJin a lot, our dating possibilities were pretty limited. For just the two of us, there were no movies, no neighborhood restaurants—no places to just hang out. The Korean CIA—which consisted of anyone's nosy parents, grandparents, and bratty younger brothers and sisters—might see us and report to Abogee. We had been going out a record two and a half months, but that meant five dates, tops.

What I liked best about her, I think, was her hair. While most of the girls we knew wore theirs long and straight or in these poodley perms, she wore hers short and shaggy. It was a mess, and it looked great on her. I liked her a lot, I have to say, and I think she liked me a lot too. Who knows what would have happened between us? I'll never know.

There's so much I'll never know. Like, if I would have been the star wing on the Alameda County soccer team this year. Manuel had introduced me to the team, a bunch of guys who'd started out playing in the garbage-strewn park by us but were now climbing up in the city ranking.

Abogee almost didn't let me play soccer. He thought it'd take too much time away from my studying and it wasn't something smart college-bound Korean boys did, only dumb wetback Latinos who ended up working in Korean stores for peanuts. You can see why Abogee and I don't always see eye to eye.

Lucky for me there were two Chinese guys on the team, Calvin and Curtis Tom. Calvin ended up going to *Yale*. I told Abogee he'd gone there on a soccer scholarship, although I wasn't sure if that was the case.

I almost didn't go to my last practice, because I was so busy packing and I was afraid it would make me too sad. But then I decided I owed it to Manuel and the team, so I went.

I was flying, at that last one. I played as hard as I had the day I tried out. By the time we quit and flopped on the ground, my blood was taking an express trip around my body, my lungs were gasping for air, and I knew I would probably never feel as happy in my whole life as I did at that moment.

Yeah.

I remember how the guys looked when Manuel told them I'd be leaving. And then how he surprised me.

A red-and-gold jersey. ALAMEDA EAGLES. Number eleven. It was beautiful.

"No one on the team will ever wear number eleven. It is always the number of our compadre Chan, *claro?*"

"*Claro.*" I ran up to Manuel and grabbed him in a bone-crunching hug. He smelled like sweat and chilies.

Then I basically ran the whole way home because I just couldn't stay there anymore.

four

I never knew there was so much wide-open space in the U.S. of A. The ribbon of highway cuts into a lot of nothing—no houses, no people, no things—all through Montana. It makes you feel like you're in an arcade game, where you're not really moving, but scenery is just passing you by: telephone poles, humps of dry grass, trees.

When we crossed into North Dakota, the nothing got even worse. We hardly saw other cars, not to mention trees, only never-ending telephone lines. A couple of times Lou strayed into the other lane, as if he were pulled by a magnet. Luckily, as I said, there were no other cars.

By the time we left Bismarck, I was ready to scream.

"We're almost there," O-Ma said. For the last few hours, the only sounds in the car had been the *plop* of fat raindrops and the *squee-squonk* of the cracked rubber wipers. We were still hours away from Minnesota.

WELCOME TO MINNESOTA, LAND OF TEN THOUSAND LAKES

"Land of Ten Thousand Hicks, I'll bet," I muttered to Young as the car crossed some unseen dotted line. "Land of Ten Thousand Hillbillies."

"I hope they have a good orchestra in Iron River," Young said, and I knew she was tired too; this was the closest she ever came to complaining.

"Want to wear my Walkman for a while?"

"Thanks, Oppa," she said, using the Korean word for older brother (I was born first). I liked it when she did that. I would call her *yohdongseng*—little sister—but it has too many syllables and I'm lazy. She shook out my Green Day tape and put in Mozart.

I watched the scenery for about the hundred thousandth time. Driving here was a huge connect-the-dots game: we hit one town, drove down a narrow highway, hit another. It wasn't anything like L.A., where you drove a couple hours to Redondo Beach on any of a zillion multilane freeways and you still never felt like you'd left the city.

I knew we were getting close when we began to see these "Adopt-a-Highway" signs that said "sponsored by Iron River such-and-such." I'm not sure how you adopt a highway—feed it, put it through college?—but I noted signs for the Iron River Rotary Club, First Lutheran Church of Iron River, Troop 17 of the Iron River Boy Scouts, the Bob (Bonnie) Gunderson family.

It was so flat around there that long before we got to town, we could see this big metal water tower sticking up. After we passed the sign IRON RIVER (POP. 7,735), we could see that the tower said in fading letters HOME OF THE MINERS/STATE FOOTBALL CHAMPS. That was the biggest thing that happened in this town in ten years. Totally lame.

O-Ma was busy studying the directions Bong had given, and she came to the conclusion that they were incomprehensible. Abogee pulled over to the side of the road, grumbling, but I saw that he was squinting at the Korean writing too. He finally steered Lou down the one street that went through town, and soon we saw a cracked sign that said IRONGATE APARTMENTS, where Bong had arranged for us to rent his old place.

Abogee shut off the car and got out. He did a few stretching exercises; I could see half-moons of sweat underneath his arms.

I was wondering why he was standing in the rain, but far be it that I should say anything.

Abogee buttoned the top buttons of his shirt, tucked the tails into his pants, cleared his throat, and farted. Young and I rolled our eyes at each other. No matter how many times we tell him that farting out loud is considered gross, he just starts in with this "If we were in Korea" bit. Let me tell you, if half his "if we were in Korea" stories are true, I don't think I'd ever want to go there.

"Chan, you come with me," he said in Korean, the very first words he'd spoken to me since we'd left.

I looked up at him. What did he need *me* for?

"Hurry! You heard me."

I clambered out of Lou. My shirt was plastered to my back. I tented it out and shook it.

We went together through a door marked OFFICE and found ourselves in a tiny, dark room. No one was there, so we sat down on chairs next to a dusty plastic fern and a wall calendar that said COMPLIMENTS OF YOUR INSURANCE AGENT, JOE NYGAARD.

The door swung open and a man lumbered in.

"Can I help you?" He was fat and bald and eying us suspiciously.

Abogee rose with a smile and extended his hand.

"I Bong Kim brudder," he said.

The man looked at the hand, but made no move to shake it. Finally Abogee took it back.

The man had beads of sweat on his upper lip; it looked the way water beads up on your car when you use Turtle Wax. I imagined him Turtle Waxing his lip, and I suddenly snorted.

"What's so funny?" the man said. Abogee glared at me. I coughed.

"I Bong Kim brudder," Abogee said again, a little more loudly.

"I can't understand a freakin' word you said." The

man turned to me. "Hey, kid, he not speak English or something?"

"Of course he does!" I said. What a jerk.

Abogee put his hand on my arm and squeezed—hard enough to make it hurt. *"I didn't give you permission to speak,"* he said.

I shut up, surprised.

"Mister," Abogee said, smiling again. "I try to tell you, I Bong Kim brud-der. You know, Bong-Ho Kim live here?"

The man squinted at Abogee. His bald head seemed to grow shinier and his cheeks puffed like Alien was going to come out of them.

"So you here to pay the money?" he growled. "The money, you know? Moolah, bread, dinero?"

"Yes, yes," Abogee said, grinning and nodding. "I pay rent."

Through the window I could see the car. Young in the back, O-Ma in the front. Both motionless as statues.

"So, where is it?" The man leaned his two hammy arms on the desk.

"Want to see room, first," Abogee said, smiling a little less.

"Uh-uh," he said. "Your brother left us without a trace—including the two months' rent he owes me."

It suddenly dawned on me what Bong had done.

"Uh, Abogee," I said. He shook his head violently and turned away from me.

"How much rent?" Abogee asked.

The man dug in a file cabinet and pulled out a sheet, while mumbling to himself, "I can't believe I let him slide. He kept saying he was gettin' money from Korea. In just a little while, please mister, just hold off a little while. Yah, right.

"Seven . . . hundred . . . fifty . . . dollars plus two . . . hundred in key money." He pronounced each digit slowly, one at a time. Abogee seemed to catch them slowly too, one at a time.

Abogee reached into a pocket and pulled out a fat envelope. He counted out nine hundred-dollar bills and a fifty.

"Abogee," I said. He gave me a warning look.

I had to do something, but I didn't know what.

"Abogee, that's Bong's rent money," I blurted in Korean.

Abogee's lips tightened.

"Quiet!" he hissed. He handed the bills to the man.

"Now, you show us room, yes?" Abogee said.

The man turned to me. "What the hell is he talking about?"

"We need to rent a place," I muttered. I let my hair fall in front of my face, as if that would shield me from what was going on.

"Hell, no!" he bellowed. "I ain't renting to no more

19

sneaks. I got what's owed and I ain't making the same mistake twice. You two better go before I get *really* mad." He made stabbing gestures at the door.

"What's going on?" Abogee asked. *"Why is he so mad? Did you insult him?"*

"He doesn't have any rooms," I explained lamely. *"He can't rent to us."*

"What? I just gave him almost a thousand dollars!"

"That was for rent Bong owed. I was trying to tell you."

"I'm gonna count to ten." The man narrowed his eyes.

"One."

"Abogee, we'd better go." I put a hand on his elbow. He pulled away.

"Mister, what going on here?" he said. "Why no rent to us? I wanna my money back."

"Two. Three . . ."

"I no leave until I get money back." Abogee sat back down on the chair, all one hundred pounds of him.

"Seven. Eight. Nine . . ."

I had a sensation of being lifted and then being forced to walk on my tippy-toes out the door. I felt a shove in my back and went flying. Luckily I had time to turn around and catch Abogee on the rebound, as he bounced off a shrub.

"And stay out, chinks!" the guy yelled, before going back into the office. The lock clicked behind him.

five

The Hell Motel was the one motel in town. It was actually the Hello Motel, but the *o* on the neon sign was flickering, almost out. We were the only people there except for the office lady, who looked like she was over a hundred years old.

She gave us a key and we went into the room, which I bet hadn't been opened for several centuries.

At least the shower worked. I felt a thousand times better after standing in there and letting the hot water beat on my back. I was a little leery of the stained, scratchy-looking towels, so I just let myself drip-dry for a bit before changing back into my clothes.

When I came out, O-Ma and Abogee were facing each other but not speaking. Young was sitting a little off to the side, on some lumpy thing that was supposed to be a couch, so I joined her.

"We have to find a place immediately," Abogee informed O-Ma. *"We don't have the money to stay in hotels like this."*

"You shouldn't have given the money to that man," O-Ma said. *"We can't keep covering for Bong's irresponsible debts."* Her voice was soft, but it seemed to slice through the gloom.

There is something about parents fighting. It's unwatchable. Young must have been thinking the same thing, because she switched on the TV. We stared at the flickering tube as if our lives depended on it.

"It is my duty to help my brother," I heard Abogee say.

"Then why don't you just send all of our money to your brother, so he can continue to waste it?" O-Ma's voice ratcheted tighter.

Young stiffened beside me. On the screen, someone was getting blown up.

"You, you—shut up!"

Young and I whirled around and stared at Abogee. His eyes were wild, and for a horrible moment I thought he was going to hit O-Ma. When his hand moved, Young sucked in her breath.

At the sound, O-Ma and Abogee turned to look at us, like they'd forgotten we were there.

Abogee's face froze, then began to collapse the slightest bit, like ice cream about to slide off a cone. But then he pulled his old face back on so fast, I couldn't exactly be sure what I had seen.

"Not in front of the children," O-Ma murmured. She sounded broken.

Young turned her face away from me and hid it under her hair, but not before I saw a tear slide down her nose.

It's weird how, when you're a kid, you think your parents can do anything: they have an answer for all your questions, they always have everything under control.

Especially Abogee. He always seemed so sure, like if he said "Jump," you'd say "How high?" But he doesn't know everything. I never realized how bad his English is. Back in L.A., Abogee got the Korean suppliers to give us their best stuff for the lowest prices—and he didn't take anyone's crap. So why did he have to smile so much while that guy was chewing us out today?

"It'll be okay," I whispered to Young.

I tried to ignore the cold feeling creeping up my gut, that maybe O-Ma and Abogee did not have everything under control, that maybe they didn't know what to do any more than Young and I did.

six

When the sun filtered through the ratty curtains, it took me a few seconds to remember where we were: the Hell Motel.

I got up, took another shower, and waited for everyone else. I always like getting up early; maybe it's because everyone else is asleep and I feel like I rule the world.

While I waited, I flipped through the Iron River phone book. I checked APARTMENTS. The Irongate Apartments were followed by another listing, the Stover Houses. For a small town, this place had a lot of apartment houses.

"O-Ma, Abogee, there's another apartment-house complex here," I said, before thinking that some people might like to sleep.

Abogee's eyes were hooded with fatigue. He looked like a lizard waking up. He sighed, looked at his watch as if we had some important appointments to keep, and said, "We might as well go see it."

We found the Stover Houses in the middle of town, catty-corner to the public library.

"Look, Young," I said. "We'll be able to walk to the library." Young is the one who likes books. I'm the one who can't live without *Sports Illustrated.*

"I like this," she said, looking up at the brick building, which had an enormous porch with all sorts of plants on it.

Abogee went in by himself. I'm sure he's convinced I did something to screw up or jinx that last visit. Last night I'd heard him murmuring to O-Ma something about how I'd spoken out of turn, how I don't respect my elders, how I'm starting to turn wild. That's me, Chan Kim, wild man.

Of course he didn't say a thing about Bong, who'd gotten us into this mess in the first place. O-Ma didn't argue with him too much. I think she was pretty tired.

Abogee came out.

"No places here," he said.

"How could that be?" I said. *"The sign says 'Rooms to let.'"*

"She said it's full." There was a warning note in his voice. I bit my tongue, although I had my suspicions that maybe our fat buddy had phoned up Mrs. Stover Houses and told her not to take us. Or maybe Mrs. Stover didn't like Koreans.

The scaredy-gut feeling clawed at me again.

Where would we go? Would we end up in rags, driving Lou endlessly through town as we scrounged for our dinner in garbage cans? Might we become Iron River's first homeless people?

"Abogee, what'll we do?" I blurted.

"Quiet! I'm trying to think." His forehead was slashed with creases.

We all stood. The silence in our conversation was punctuated only by the twittering of birds.

"We should try chamber of commerce," O-Ma said finally, clearly and brightly in English.

"Huh! What that gonna do?" Abogee challenged her.

"They know where businesses are," O-Ma reasoned. I was surprised to see her turn around and walk into the Stover Houses without even pretending to wait for Abogee's approval.

She came back out and pointed in the direction of the library. "On Main Street; we can walk. Mrs. Stover said okay to keep car here."

Abogee grumbled, but he led the way.

I noticed, as we passed the library, that it didn't have one little streak of graffiti on it. Not a one. This town was like a movie set.

The chamber of commerce looked like an advertising hut. Banners for the Kiwanis and Rotary clubs adorned the desk, where a lady sat expectantly. A poster on the wall touted a summer boat show up at some Whatchamagoober Lake. On another wall hung a framed etching of what looked like the Grand Canyon but was labeled STEAM SHOVEL MINE, 1898.

"Hello," the lady said. "Can I help you?"

Abogee was about to say something, but O-Ma gracefully inserted herself.

"Hello, I am Ok-Hee Kim and this is my family. We are new here, and we need place to live for a while."

The lady was wearing those glasses with the tiny lenses that made it seem like you needed tiny eyes to look through them. She smiled. Her smile seemed kind.

"Have you tried the Irongate Apartments or the Stover Houses?" she asked. "Both are very nice."

"Oh yes, they very nice," O-Ma said. "But we look for something little bit cheaper and maybe less like hotel, you know?"

"Oh, of course," the lady said, opening up a small box of index cards. "Mrs. Evie Knutson has been looking for someone to rent the top floor of her house for some time since her husband died. Let me copy down the address for you."

Mrs. Knutson's house turned out to be exactly across the street from the library. Hers was a large, slightly dilapidated place. The lawn was overgrown with weeds that were choking the ROOM FOR RENT sign.

"You get car," O-Ma said to us. "I go talk to Mrs. Knutson."

We drove our bucket of bolts into an alley in order to reach the driveway in the back of the house. Through the screen door, O-Ma's voice tinkled gently, like wind chimes.

We knocked, and a warbly voice told us to come in. O-Ma was sitting at a table talking to an elderly lady whose white hair was tucked in a neat bun. She looked like Grandma Moses.

"What a lovely family!" she gushed, extending her hand to Abogee. He looked bewildered and took her hand very gently, as if she were handing him a baby bird.

"You have a lovely daughter and a very handsome boy," she said to O-Ma, who smiled. She gave Young and me each a butterscotch candy.

The next thing I knew, I was lugging the Buddha and our boxes up a flight of lopsided stairs. Upstairs there were two rooms, a big one and a small one. Abogee started throwing Young's and my stuff in the small one, which smelled faintly of mothballs.

"There's a room in the attic," he said. *"Mrs. Knutson said it's drafty, but Chan, you can sleep up there, if you want."*

Young and I peered closer at the room before us. I could almost touch the opposite walls if I spread my arms. There were shelves already built on one wall. I couldn't help wondering if Mrs. Knutson used it as a closet. We looked at each other again and then went to search for the attic.

There was a rope hanging from the ceiling, and when I pulled on it, a door with stairs built into it emerged. It was like a reverse trapdoor.

"Cool," said Young as I unfolded the stairs.

The attic was unfinished: on half of it, insulation covered the boards like a carpet of pink cotton candy. The other half was clear, but looked like it hadn't been swept out since the Civil War. Shadows of miscellaneous junk lurked ominously in the corners.

"Don't feel like you have to sleep up here," Young said.

Actually, I was thinking that this place might be decent, relatively speaking. I had a sudden hunger for my own space.

"I'll try my luck here, Sis."

I would have made a good monk: I have very few possessions. I carried my stuff up in one trip, piled it on an old overstuffed chair, and swept out the floor with a broom and dustpan that Mrs. Knutson gave me. O-Ma came up later with some oil soap, saying she wanted to make sure it was really clean, since I'd be sleeping on it. We didn't have beds. O-Ma and Abogee had decided that we would just bring all our quilts and sleep Korean style, maybe buy furniture later.

"This isn't so bad, is it?" she asked. She smoothed the hair falling into my eyes just the way she'd smoothed the bedding a few minutes ago.

I suddenly wanted to tell O-Ma how proud I was about how she had handled everything today. But as always, when I want to say something nice, something totally stupid and whiny comes out.

"I wish we had our own place."

"So do I. But don't you think this is a nice way to get started? Mrs. Knutson seems so kind."

"But we don't even have a kitchen."

"Mrs. Knutson has a nice one, downstairs."

"You're going to share?"

"We'll work something out," O-Ma said.

"You're good at working things out," I said, relieved that I finally said something positive.

"I think I'll try to learn to cook more American food," she said determinedly. *"Now, you be good and help your father, okay?"*

"Okay," I said. O-Ma crept down the stairs and pushed them back up. The springs snapped the door tightly back into place, and the room went black.

I lay in the warm blanket of darkness, smelling the faint scent of oil soap. Our future was outside, leaning black and heavy against the house. It scared me, but I didn't know what to do about it.

seven

The next day O-Ma took us to register for school. We went in Lou, because the school was on the edge of town. That was the problem with Iron River: since there was nothing other than prairie out here, it seemed the town thought it might as well spread out.

Iron River High School was actually in an imposing building. It had columns outside the front door like the Parthenon, and a huge lawn that some poor soul had obviously taken a good deal of care in mowing. There was also a track, a football field, and tennis courts.

The inside of the school was like something preserved for a museum: floors waxed and gleaming, rows of shiny lockers, not a single one bent or graffitied. At El Caldero High, such a sight would've been considered a miracle, like when the face of Jesus appeared in a tortilla this lady was frying.

"Much cleaner than your old school, don't you think?" O-Ma asked us in English. I could tell she was practicing up for meeting the principal. She looked calm, but the hand that clutched the folder with our school records was a hand with a mission. You couldn't have pried that thing away from her.

We followed the trophy cases, which contained rows of gleaming trophies and framed pictures of sports teams, plaques in the shape of Minnesota. We found the door marked PRINCIPAL and bumped into the big man himself, Mr. Ripanen. His office was right there when you came in—you didn't have to be admitted through several sets of doors like at our school.

"Hello, hello, the Kim family," he boomed, extending his hands in welcome.

"Yes, I was the one who call earlier," O-Ma said, almost shyly.

"Come in, come in," he said, ushering us into the office. We let O-Ma sit closest to him. He had a poster that said IT TAKES A VILLAGE TO RAISE A CHILD over his desk. SuJin would love it, I was thinking.

Young's school report caught his eye right away.

"Young has a great record," he said, looking from me to her, as if he were trying to figure out which was which. I know we looked alike as babies—the same hair that stuck up like a mad scientist's, the same black-comma eyes—but this was ridiculous.

"Let's see, just about straight A's, a few—just a few—math awards." He leaned back in his chair, a finger to his lips as if he were trying to keep a laugh or something inside.

"She was first runner-up in the state math contest," O-Ma volunteered. "And she was just accepted into L.A. Young People's Orchestra."

He seemed slightly relieved, and wheeled his chair to face Young head-on. He asked her about her interests, and she said she'd like to find an orchestra as well as get in some higher-level math courses, since she had already taken trig.

"We have a very good marching band," Mr. Ripanen said. "They've played all over the state." Young smiled politely. I think for her the idea of playing her precious silver flute in some band was about as inviting as mud wrestling. "And we'll see about those classes."

"And you're Chan," he said to me. I wasn't sure if that was a question, but I nodded my head to be on the safe side. He scanned my record. I'm pretty much a B/occasional-A student, but let me tell you, that still requires an effort.

"Very good," he said diplomatically. He asked me what my interests were. I didn't know what to say. I didn't want to sound like a moron next to Young.

"I like to read," I said finally, even though both Young and O-Ma were looking at me in surprise. "I'm glad we live by the library."

"Good, good," Mr. Ripanen said heartily. "Good to

be a reader. My son's a reader, absolutely *loves* books."

I was thinking about mentioning soccer, but after he said that, I decided that his kid was probably a geek, so I shouldn't risk upsetting him. For a guy that big to have a geeky kid, that must be a drag. Besides, O-Ma and Abogee—especially Abogee—have never counted sports as a legit school activity.

"Anyone can build muscle," Abogee would say, pointing to his arm. Then he'd point to his head. *"But building brain, that's much tougher."*

"And what about school bus?" O-Ma asked.

Mr. Ripanen looked puzzled.

"What about it?"

"Where do children pick it up?"

Mr. Ripanen still looked puzzled. "You live on Howard Street, by the library, right?"

O-Ma nodded.

"There isn't a bus." Mr. Ripanen looked amused.

"But it's so far," O-Ma protested.

"The only kids who get bus service are the ones in Neeshawatin, which is almost an hour away. You should see what a headache it is getting them here when it snows."

So Young and I were going to walk to school every day, rain, shine—or snow. Argh. I know most people think Californians jump in their car to visit their next-door neighbors, but that's an exaggeration. We were a mile from school. *Definitely* driving distance.

"You're less than a mile from the school," Mr. Ripanen said, as if my thoughts were broadcast on a billboard. "I'd say it's less than three-quarters of a mile. And it's good to walk. Kids don't get enough exercise these days."

Oh, yeah? And what about your geeky son?

O-Ma accepted all this gracefully. "Okay, if they supposed to walk, they walk."

"We'll have something to tell our grandkids," Young added cheerfully. I wanted to pinch her.

Mr. Ripanen informed us that Young and I would be entering eleventh grade, right on schedule.

"Chan, Young, I need you to help me start cleaning up the store," Abogee announced. *"We will begin immediately after lunch."*

Mrs. Knutson offered us some Spam sandwiches. At first O-Ma and Abogee declined—no, no, too much trouble; we don't want to eat up your food—but the third time Mrs. Knutson offered, they pounced. Abogee said to us that Spam is considered a delicacy in Korea. Young gave me a look. *We* knew Spam was made of rodent parts.

Mrs. Knutson looked pleased. "Spam is made right here in Minnesota," she said. "There's plenty to go around."

After lunch Young and I sat around waiting for Abogee. There was no sound coming in from the open window except for the occasional purr of a car, the chirp of a bird. No clanking, honking, or cursing. No sirens, no *whoosh-creak* of a bus going by. It was just . . . nothing.

Weird.

"You know what? I think Abogee's taking a nap."

I strained my ears. Sure enough, there was a slight breathing noise coming from the bedroom, regular as ocean waves.

"That's a new one."

Young looked worried. "I know. It's not like him." She hesitated. "I wonder if I'll have to sell my flute."

"What?" Young's flute is a solid-silver number that cost a couple hundred bucks.

"Do you have a drug habit you haven't told me about?"

"Oppa, this is serious," she said. "I have a feeling money's going to be kind of tight around here."

"When hasn't it been tight?" Once, Abogee had chewed us out because he thought we were wasting toilet paper. He rationed us to three squares per dump. Unbelievable. O-Ma gave Young and me some money to buy extra rolls on the sly.

"Listen, Sis. I'm sure we got a fair sum of money from selling the store."

"Abogee loaned Bong a lot of money to buy this one. We aren't making anything now."

"Hey, kid, it'll be all right." I put my arm around her. "Your oppa will make sure of that."

Of course, I was worried too. It's cheaper to live in the boonies, but you're also going to have fewer customers. And it's not like O-Ma and Abogee's friends are around to give us things like they used to: fresh fish from Mr. Lee's fishing boat, bags of rice, clothes from the ones who owned stores. I got my favorite soccer shorts from Mr. Park, Abogee's best friend. I picked them out myself.

"Oppa, I'm scared," Young said, her eyes all liquidy like a puppy's.

"It'll be all right, Young." I stopped to listen to myself. What slim pickings in my big-brother repertoire. I took a breath.

"Okay, then let's do something. Maybe *we* need to take charge. Let's wake Abogee up and get him on the ball."

Young gave me a look, like, *I dare you*.

I went upstairs.

Abogee was sleeping on the Korean quilt, the one that had patterns of dragons on it. He slept neatly, his arms close to his sides like a soldier. Their room, never big to begin with, looked even smaller with all the stuff crammed in. From the corner the Buddha statue grinned at me from under a stack of legal-looking papers.

Next to the bed was Abogee's Bible. Back in L.A. he'd always kept it next to the bed too.

For some reason I picked it up. I looked at the gilt embossed on the cover and realized that even though I knew the Korean word for Bible, *Songkyong*, I had no idea what it looked like written, had no idea which of these clusters of letters spelled it out.

I opened the book. The text was split in two columns: English on one side, Korean on the other. There were some notations in Korean, on both sides. The writing was faded and wispy, as if it had been painted on by spider legs. On Sunday mornings, even though Abogee didn't have time to go to church, he was always up early with a cup of coffee, studying the Bible. He'd translate the Korean to English and then check himself with the English version.

What I remember, too, was whenever there was a lull at the Extravaganza, he'd pull out his Korean-English dictionary and just read it, like he was reading a book.

A thought suddenly occurred to me. Was this how he taught himself English?

I would've given a lot to know what the writing in the margins said. I guess I would've given a lot to know *anything*, only I didn't want to have to ask him. Sounds crazy, doesn't it?

Abogee's snores went up, then down. *SNARK!-wheeze. SNARK!-wheeze.* His forehead was creased, as if he had to concentrate on staying asleep. I put the Bible gently back in its place and left the room.

When Abogee appeared at dinner, he looked like he'd just come out of a coma. Young and I didn't say a thing. He and O-Ma went to bed early.

eight

When I saw the all the kids walking up the lawn, con-verging at the brick school building, my heart went from its normal *lub-dub, lub-dub* to *lub-dubdubdub, lub-dubdubdub.*

A bunch of girls in T-shirts that said IRON RIVER CHEERLEADERS were practicing jumps and pyramids on the front lawn. They stopped and stared as Young and I went by.

The kids looked normal enough, like kids, anyway, but I finally figured out what was weird.

They were all blond.

Blond beyond California blond. Albino blond. Some had hair so light you practically couldn't see individual strands, like their hair was molded out of butter. I strained to catch a glimpse of the familiar black hair and black eyes of the Asian or Mexican kids. Or the dark skin of the black kids. Nope. It was a complete whiteout.

Young was staring too.

"Do you think people will know we're twins?" she asked. Her voice quavered a little.

"We *do* look alike, don't we?" I said. My own voice sounded thin, like it was cracking around the edges. Man, I had to do better than this. My own little sister was taking this better than I was.

My first class was biology. I trudged to the room on the second floor, took a deep breath, and walked in.

Everyone got really quiet.

I took a seat in the back and instinctively reached for the bill of my baseball cap—which wasn't there. At my old school I wore my L.A. Dodgers hat all the time. I could hide under it if I wanted to daydream. I wouldn't have minded hiding under it now.

But no more. There's a *dress code* here. No hats, shorts, open-toe sandals, midriff-baring tops, and other things I can't remember. Unbelievable. The closest our old school came to that was when they said you couldn't wear gang-related stuff.

I snuck a look at the guy next to me and noticed that *he* was wearing a T-shirt with a dazed smiley face that said GET HIGH on it. Then I saw how he was staring at me.

Everyone was staring. Okay, so I'm a two-headed mutant rhino, so thick-skinned that I won't notice if you gawk. I tried to act like I didn't care.

I'm a lousy actor.

The door opened and a tall skinny man who looked like Prince Charles charged into the room.

"Sorry I'm late, class," he said, glancing at the wall clock. "As you've probably figured out, I'm Mr. Minsky, your biology teacher."

He looked at a sheet of paper waiting on his desk.

"Chan Jung Kim. New student. Did I say your name right?"

I nodded. I guess it didn't take too much for him to figure I was the new guy. "Please call me Chan."

"Okay. Welcome to Iron River High School. Class, give a hand to your new classmate, Chan Kim." Everyone clapped listlessly.

I was a little disappointed that Mr. Minsky didn't mention I was from L.A. He just told us to put covers on our textbooks.

I had to do this hello-I'm-Chan-I'm-new-thanks-for-the-applause routine for three more classes and then it was lunch. In that time, no one had come up to me offering to be my best buddy, so I was going to have to sit alone. That's what happens when you're new.

It made it a billion times worse, the way everyone was blabbering on excitedly to everyone—How was your summer? Did you see so-and-so?—just the way I'd be if I were back home. Crud. Now I didn't even know where the stupid lunchroom was.

I saw this guy coming from the opposite direction.

Blond, no surprise, but he was wearing Adidas Sambas turf shoes. Soccer shoes. The first I'd seen here.

He looked like a player, the way he moved, shoulders flat out, arms curved but ready at his side. Maybe even a wing—he had that look, right down to his ALL-PRO T-shirt.

"Yo!" I said. I don't know what possessed me. "Know where the lunchroom is?"

He gestured vaguely in the direction I'd been heading, then he moved on.

From down the hall I could hear the noise. Dishes clanking, voices at a low-key roar. I imagined sitting by myself, eating, and having a bunch of strangers watch me do it. Maybe I'd find Young. Great. We could eat alone together.

Forget this. I wasn't going to play by the rules of Hicksville High. I was going to find a quiet place by myself to chew on my sandwich.

I turned and took the opposite corridor to its end. A sign pointed to the gym. What the heck. I crossed a tiny indoor running track and went in.

A bunch of guys, including ALL-PRO, were sitting on the bleachers. Most of them looked like your typical jocks. A couple of them were in black shirts and shredded jeans, like the metalheads at my old school. Except that at El Caldero, the metalheads were all skinny heroin-addicts-in-training. Every one of these guys was huge, like a lumberjack.

They all stopped talking and stared at me as I walked in.

"Who the hell are you?" said a guy whose muscles jumped like shot-put balls under his black Megadeth T-shirt. He had dirty blond hair that hung in quasi-Rasta clumps like a mop.

"Who wants to know?"

"I wanna know. When Rom asks, you answer, weeg."

I wasn't exactly sure what a weeg was, but I figured it wasn't anything good, since the guy next to him started to laugh like a hyena. This guy's hair and eyes were dark; he looked almost Mexican. I found myself staring at him, trying to figure out what he was.

"Hey, new guy," said ALL-PRO. "Where ya from?"

"L.A."

The guys, collectively, all sort of went "*Hmm*." Like this development was slightly interesting to them.

But I wasn't going to stand around for them. I went to a corner of the gym, sat on a bench, and inhaled my sandwich. I hadn't brought anything to drink, so the peanut butter practically strangled me on the way down.

Young and I walked home together. For about three blocks we didn't say anything. Then we both started talking at once: "Howwasit?" "Whatdidyouthink?"

"You first," Young said.

"No, ladies first."

"It sucked."

"Same."

We walked.

"Everyone is about as friendly as cacti," I said, thinking specifically of the guys at lunch. "Like they have so much to feel superior about. Iron River, home of an iron mine, state football champs when I was in kindergarten. Whoopee."

Young took a breath.

"Some girl called me 'pancake face' in the hall."

"Whoa—" I said. "What was that all about?"

Young shrugged. Her shoulder blades pointed out from under her shirt like wings. "I think she meant my face is flat." She pushed her hand in close to her face, as if measuring it.

"Your face isn't flat," I said, fuming. "That girl's brain is flat." Jesus. My sister gets insulted by a bigoted yahoo on our first day of school. That's all I needed to hear.

When we got home, there was a smell of cookies baking. We could hear Mrs. Knutson saying to O-Ma, "So you just flatten 'em out with a fork like this after you dip 'em in sugar to get that crisscrossy pattern. Easy, yah?"

Young and I had warm cookies—something we'd never had before because O-Ma was always busy working—and we felt a little better.

nine

Another afternoon of nothing awaited. Back in L.A., O-Ma and Abogee had started making me go to these after-school *hakwon* to bone up for the SATs. In between that I had soccer practice, and on weekends I worked at the store. That was then. Now I watched *Oprah,* and when I got tired of that I went outside and kicked the soccer ball around for a while. I practiced some of the passes Manuel had taught me, but it's not so easy to do with just one person. I hated to admit it, but I was almost hoping for some homework.

I didn't even have any small projects, like putting covers on my books. O-Ma had made these great denim ones for both me and Young on Mrs. Knutson's sewing machine. It was cool seeing my old jeans on my books, but I don't know where she got the time to do it—she seemed to be running around so much all day and all night.

So was Abogee. Each day he was gone by the time Young and I ate breakfast, and he didn't come home until dinner, which we had extra late, just for him. And every night he just came home and ate, no progress reports, no nothing.

Maybe he could use some help. I changed my clothes and walked downtown.

Our store was called Froggie's Express, and it was nestled between a Singer sewing machine store and Koski's Pharmacy. I went through the door, which was open, even though the sign said CLOSED, and found Abogee standing behind a grimy counter. He was sweating, but it was hard to see exactly what he'd been doing because the store looked like Godzilla had come shopping: boxes upturned on the floor, shelves standing bare while others looked like they'd been pulled down. In the middle of it all was a pile of crumbling cinder blocks.

"Do you need help with anything?" I asked. Abogee snapped out of whatever trance he was in and regarded me.

"Is all your homework done?"

I nodded.

"You can move some of those blocks to the back if you want." He gestured to the door that went out the back. *"There are some gloves on the hook over there."*

I put on the white cotton gloves with rubber gripper dots, the kind of gloves that every Korean grocer uses. I would have liked to know how the blocks ended up in the middle of the floor in the first place, but Abogee

47

didn't look like he was in a storytelling mood.

In a few minutes I was sweating too, but it felt good. My blood was totally pumping with the effort. I could always count on my body to rise to the occasion whenever I needed to lift, or kick, or hit.

At one point I took a break. Abogee was watching me. When he saw me looking at him, he turned away.

I wanted to ask him if he was worried. It didn't make sense that we'd have to give up everything to run a store in some weird town where everyone was blond. The Extravaganza had been going great guns, but Young had been right. I'd overheard O-Ma mention something to Abogee about the low price we'd gotten for it because we needed to leave so quickly.

How *were* we doing financially? That's not exactly the kind of question you bring up in casual conversation.

"That is enough for today," Abogee said, after I dragged the last block out. His shoulders were bent, like he had an enormous weight pressing on them. *"Thank you for your help."*

How're you doing, Abogee? The words were sitting right on my tongue, but at the last minute I swallowed them. Abogee would probably get angry if I asked, like I was questioning his authority, his Abogee-ness.

I stepped over a crumpled box on the way out. I didn't want to leave Abogee to worry all by himself, but I didn't know what else to do.

ten

Call me a masochist, but I kept going to the gym to eat lunch. I liked it there, even though the other guys ignored me.

I'd figured out their story. Almost all of them had Iron River football letter jackets, even the metalheads. They also acted like typical football players: talking loud, punching each other, saying "Duh" a lot.

The biggest guy, the one who gave me the who-the-hell-are-you? Welcome Wagon treatment on the first day, was the biggest fool. His favorite trick was stomping hard on a full container of milk—which was great fun for all involved, except for the poor janitorial slob who would have to clean it up later. His buddy, the hyena boy, laughed uproariously at anything the Monster did. I hate guys like that.

The ALL-PRO guy was about the only one who would directly stand up to Monster—and the Monster guy actually seemed to listen. Once, when ALL-PRO and I passed in the halls, he nodded to me. Or maybe that's just the way he walked.

In biology Mr. Minsky made us sign a card for some football player, Gary Lindstrom, who was in the hospital.

At lunch I overheard the guys talking about his accident. Gary had just gotten his driver's license, and on his maiden voyage he'd pulled a too-quick left onto the highway, right into the path of another car.

Now, apparently, he was lying in a hospital bed with a concussion and both legs smashed up. A couple of the guys made jokes about him having sex with a nurse. But things were quieter, queasier, than they were normally.

"Hey!" ALL-PRO yelled across the gym, toward the end of lunch.

"Hey!" he yelled again. "Yo! Yo, kid!"

I chewed my sandwich slowly. There was no mistaking who he was yelling at.

"What?" I finally said.

"C'mere."

All the guys were looking at me. What else was there to do? I walked over there, as if this were the showdown at the OK Corral.

"Hey, kid."

"My name's Chan," I said. There was a sour taste in my mouth.

"Chan. You play soccer, am I right?"

I shrugged.

"I saw you playing out in your yard once," ALL-PRO said. "Look, our kicker is out for the season. We need a guy to take his place. Think you might be able to kick a football?"

"Why don't *you* do it?" I said to him, looking at his Sambas. I mean, what kind of question was that? A soccer ball is nothing like a football, as any moron will tell you. Besides, the guy was a player already.

ALL-PRO laughed, lifted up his feet like he was just now discovering he had them. "Are you talking about these? I got 'em on a trip to Minneapolis. I like how they look."

"We don't have soccer up here," growled Monster. "Soccer is for fags."

"Fine," I said. And football was for overfed idiots. I had no idea what the purpose of this conversation was, anyway. I turned around and made for the exit.

"No, wait!" ALL-PRO jumped off the benches and trotted up to me, keeping pace.

"I'm Mikko," he said.

"What kind of name is that?" I couldn't help saying. "It sounds Japanese."

He frowned. "What kind of name is Chan? It sounds stupid."

"Sorry," I said.

"It's okay. It's Finnish. Lucky for me—my mom's Swedish and she wanted to name me Olaf."

51

I laughed, despite myself. "Mine's Korean."

We kept walking together. In fact, we passed Young, who beamed at me, probably thinking I had found a friend.

"Why don't you try out? I think you'd be good."

"Yeah, I can tell how much you want me for your team by the way you treat me so nice at lunch."

He gave me this puzzled look, like maybe he didn't get it.

"Aw, come on," he said after a minute. "It always takes time for new guys."

I shrugged. "I'm not interested, *comprendes?*"

ALL-PRO kept trotting alongside me.

"But you're interested in playing *something*, aren't you? There aren't a lot of sports to pick from here. Most guys I know would kill to get a shot at a varsity spot on the football team."

I nodded, as if I really cared. I opened my locker and started gathering up my books.

"The guys on the team are good guys. I mean, some of them can be jerks, but they're mostly okay."

I didn't trust him. I didn't trust anyone here.

"What's in it for me?" I said finally.

He gave me a look. "Well, if you play anything, you know what the reward is. It's playing. Doesn't hurt with the chicks, either."

Chicks. Where were these people from—the seventies? Young and I once asked Mrs. Knutson why she didn't have an answering machine, and she said, "What's an answering machine?" Iron River was the Town Time Forgot.

"I'll think about it," I said, just as I noticed that the halls were deserted. The bell rang. ALL-PRO didn't move.

My sense of the law was getting the better of me. "I think we'd better go."

"Hey, it's no problem." Mikko rooted around in his pockets until he produced a Pepto-Bismol-pink slip.

"My dad's the principal. Give this to the teacher, and she won't hassle you."

By the time I looked up to say "Thanks," ALL-PRO was already way down the hall, walking in his coiled-animal kind of way while looking as if he had all the time in the world.

It was weird to think he was the closest thing I had to a friend here.

eleven

"He said you should come to practice," ALL-PRO said, shadowing me after lunch. Jesus, he was persistent. He stayed with me all the way to my locker.

"Who says what?" I gathered my books.

"The coach. I got him to okay a late tryout," ALL-PRO said impatiently. "Can you come today? I tried to call you last night, but I didn't know your last name."

"It's Kim," I said. I tried to think of a fast way to get out of this. "I don't have any gym clothes with me."

"You get the stuff issued," ALL-PRO said. "Not to worry."

"Oh," was all I could think to say, which he seemed to take as a yes.

He grinned and slapped my shoulder. "Meet you in the locker room after school."

The bell rang. My last class was over. I thought about what there was to do at home. Nothing. Not even homework. The show on *Oprah* was going to be on people who remarry their ex-spouses.

So I called home and told O-Ma I'd be staying late for a school activity. Then I headed to the locker room.

There were two doors. One said VARSITY, the other, JUNIOR VARSITY. I stood there for a second, then pushed open the VARSITY door. What the hell.

Both doors led into the same room.

It was like entering a beehive. Guys were busy suiting up, taping things. Pads lay like discarded insect parts all over the floor. No one looked up when I came in.

"You Jann Kim?" asked a man with a military bearing and a shiny whistle around his neck. He looked like the kind of guy who didn't like to be corrected. So I didn't.

"Uh, yeah."

"Mike Thorson. Head coach." He extended his hand and shook hard, squeezing my fingers to Silly Putty. The guy was tan, almost Manuel's natural color. But his blue eyes, pale as sea glass, gave away his background. Son of Thor.

"Mikko Ripanen says you play soccer."

I nodded.

"Good." He laid a paw on my shoulder. "As you probably know, our kicker is out of commission."

"I know. I'm sorry." His hand felt strange on my shoulder. It wasn't something Abogee would do.

"We're glad you're here, though," Coach said. "What size are you, clothes and shoes?"

He came back with an armload of pads, a helmet, cleats, and a uniform. He dumped everything on the bench just as ALL-PRO walked in, slapping me on the back and grinning a mile wide, like he'd just caught a fish or something.

"Ripanen, an extra mile after practice. You can't just breeze in anytime you want."

"Sorry, Coach, my stagecoach got a flat tire." ALL-PRO winked at me. "Besides, you know I always do extra."

Coach growled, but he didn't really seem mad.

"Glad you made it," ALL-PRO said as I studied the mess of stuff in front of me. "It's our first full-pad workout today."

"Uh-huh," I said knowingly. There were enough pads here to build another Chan. Or Jann.

"Here," he said, tossing me a gray T-shirt that was so worn, it was the consistency of spiderwebs. "This goes on first, to mop up the sweat and the stink."

ALL-PRO showed me how to put my hip and kidney pads into this kinky thing called a girdle. Sliding the tight football pants over that was like putting the casing on a sausage. Next came the shoulder and elbow pads and then a practice jersey over that.

On our way out I caught a glance of myself, fully padded, in the mirror. For the first time in my life, I looked huge. As in HUGE. Then ALL-PRO came up from behind. Next to him I looked dorkily small again. I decided I needed to start lifting.

"Come on, you dirtbags! You're holding everyone up!"

"That's Kearny," said ALL-PRO. "The assistant coach."

We trotted over to the rest of the guys. Monster and another guy were leading everyone in stretches. Half the guys couldn't even touch their toes. Thanks to my tae kwon do training, I could push my palms to the grass.

Kearny looked at me funny when he walked by, like maybe having excellent hamstrings wasn't such a good thing for a football player. I don't know.

"M-I-N-E-R-S! Hut! Hut! Hut!"

We did jumping jacks, which is no easy task when you're wearing what feels like fifty pounds of equipment. Beads of sweat began to roll down my back.

"Helmets on!" Coach barked. ALL-PRO helped me adjust the pads on mine. The strap made my chin itch. I felt like I was descending into a hot and sweaty bell.

"Go to the dummy! Go to the dummy! Go to the dummy!"

Everything echoed.

The dummy, an upright punching bag mounted on a heavy base, bulged where it was patched messily with electrical tape.

57

"Kill it!" Kearny commanded.

A guy slammed into the dummy and pushed it all over the field. The next guy managed to keep pushing it at a run.

"Faster! Harder! Push it!" Kearny screamed.

My turn. I took a breath, ran, and crashed head-on into it. It barely budged.

Was that a snicker back in the line?

"What are you, a girl?" Kearny yelled. "Put some muscle behind it!"

I backed up and charged again. *Oof.* My pads crunched into my shoulders as I pushed.

"Run *through* it!" Kearny yelled. He yanked me aside. "Like this!" He smashed into it, without pads, and moved it a good ten feet.

I tried again.

"That's better!"

We did more drills, then we scrimmaged. The Mexican-looking guy, Monster's friend, did the kickoff. I went in a couple times to play running back.

Then Coach lined us up in the end zone, in two rows. He gave each of us a shield-size pad, just like the ones we used in tae kwon do to practice kicks.

"We're gonna let Ripanen run first, 'cause he's the biggest wiseguy," Kearny cackled. "A little bit of necessary roughness to cut that big mouth down a notch or two."

"Yah, you're on!" ALL-PRO smirked, throwing his pad to the ground. Kearny picked it up.

ALL-PRO backed up about thirty feet, a ball under his arm.

"Ready, hosers?" he called.

"You're gonna die, you weeg," said Monster.

ALL-PRO just laughed.

He came up fast in between the lines, like a bull running after a cape. Everyone leaned in to clobber him. He slowed but kept on driving. Then Kearny leaned in for a full body-blow; someone else smashed him on the head.

ALL-PRO breathed heavily, grunted, but then broke free, still with the ball.

"Nice try, losers," he said, waving the ball at us. He grabbed a pad, vengeance in his eyes.

"Next?"

My turn. I rammed through, falling once, but didn't lose the ball, as some of the others did. I managed to get out, practically crawling on all fours. Man, I wished I was as big as Monster. He just basically strolled through the lines as if he was taking his Sunday constitutional or something. No one came close to stopping him.

"All right." Coach looked at his watch. "Line up. We're letting you off easy today."

"Sprints," ALL-PRO explained to me as we were

herded to the opposite end zone. "Coaches make us do this till someone pukes."

"No talking!" Coach yelled, his whistle clenched between his teeth. "I want you to sprint to the fifty, bearwalk back, four times. And quick. Anyone muck up, we start all over again."

The whistle screamed.

We ran, then lumbered back on our hands and feet, butts high in the air ("No knees!" Kearny yelled at me) like very ungainly bears. My arms and legs were lead. Blood rushed to my head.

"Faster! Quit lagging, Beargrease! Push it!"

Sprint down, thirty push-ups, sprint back.

"Do it, Janovich. Keep going!"

Sprint down, fifty sit-ups, sprint back.

"Come on, Leland! This isn't afternoon tea!"

Heat and blood filled my head. My abs burned as I convulsed like a pitiful bug on its back. Forty sit-ups to go, oxygen debt at its max.

Ju keh ta, I found myself thinking. I'm going to die.

Then I heard the noise—*"hai-yaargh!"*

Monster, on all fours as if he was going to play horsie with a little kid, ejected about a bucket and a half of puke.

"Okay, gentlemen," Coach said. "Hit the showers."

"Man, Rom, what'd you have for lunch—rubber erasers?" said his buddy, bending over Monster, who was sitting there with his head between his knees. A few feet away his barf pooled in the grass. The ground refused to take it.

"So how'd you like it?" ALL-PRO asked me.

"It was okay." Every muscle—including those in my eyeballs—felt like it had been dipped in salt water and wrung out like beef jerky. It felt good in a bad way and vice versa, if you know what I mean.

"How come I didn't get to kick? I thought that's why you wanted me."

"Uh-uh," he said. "First, we need to see if you can take it, the football part. This is nine-man ball. Kicker has to do more than kick."

"So how'd I do?"

Mikko paused and looked at me, as if he was trying to figure out what to say. Something grabbed my stomach. All of a sudden I wanted to hear him say he thought I could do it.

He shrugged. "You obviously haven't played football before." He shrugged again. "You have a *lot* of work to do, learning plays and stuff like that. But I think you can take it."

I found myself grinning. That was enough.

twelve

The next day I was crippled. And I was happy as a clam. There's something purifying about pushing your body to its limits and then just surrendering to the tiredness that fills in every crack. Even though I needed a wheelchair, my brain felt clearer than it had in ages, like it did after a hard tae kwon do workout or a tough soccer game.

"Why are you walking so funny?" O-Ma asked as I helped get out the cereal and milk.

"Getting old," I said. Mrs. Knutson wandered into the kitchen in a furry pink robe, groping for coffee.

Young ran down, her flute in hand.

"I'm going to Donna's house to practice flute after school," she said, grabbing her lunch.

"Donna is that girl from math class?" O-Ma called to her.

"Yes!" Young said. Her voice faded as she flew out the door.

"O-Ma, I think I'm going to stay after school again today."

"Chotta," she said, which basically means fine and dandy. "What are you up to?"

"Um, some kids are starting a club." I wasn't exactly sure why I didn't want to tell her. Maybe it was because I didn't want to jinx it.

"Just be home for dinner at seven."

"Okay."

As usual, Abogee was already at the store.

"Hey, Chan!" ALL-PRO yelled at lunch. "Come sit with us."

I threw my sandwich into my bag and suppressed an idiotic grin.

"Hey," said eighty percent of the guys when I sat down. Monster and the Mexican-looking guy didn't say anything. But I didn't care. It felt good to have a group to eat with.

"You ever kicked a football before?" Coach asked me.

"No," I said honestly. The closest I'd ever come was a Nerf at the beach.

"Shouldn't be a problem. You seem quick," he said, clapping a hand on my shoulder pad. "Beargrease here will show you the particulars."

Jimmi Beargrease was the black-haired kid, friend to

Monster. I guess he wasn't Mexican, but Indian. Today his long hair stuck out in a braid under his helmet. He scowled when Coach told him to help me out.

"Here," he said, shoving a football and a tee at me. He had terrible teeth, all yellow and crooked. "You put the football on this."

I took the stuff from him. "I said I'd never kicked before, not that I'm retarded." That came out a little harsher than I meant it to, but I wasn't that sorry. There are some guys that you just don't like right off the bat, and he was one of them.

He didn't say anything. He loped up to the ball and booted it, fairly decent, about twenty yards.

I reset it; regarded it. Then I ran up and kicked. It took to the air, changed its mind, crashed down, bounced, and came to rest like a dead animal a few yards away.

"Nice," Jimmi said sarcastically. He glanced over his shoulder to make sure I saw what he saw: that Coach was watching.

I tried again. Same result.

"Maybe you're not cut out to be a kicker," Jimmi said helpfully.

I reset the ball.

You know how to kick, I told myself. Focus. I ran, keeping my knee over the ball, thinking, GOAL!

The ball took off, a bit drunkenly. But it kept on

going and sailed about forty yards before falling plumply back down.

"Whoo-ee!" came a cry from the field. ALL-PRO, arm raised mid-pass, gave me the V-for-victory sign. "Way to go, Chanster! Look at that leg!"

"Nice," said Jimmi. He was trying to be sarcastic and failing miserably.

"You look happy, young man," said Mrs. Knutson at dinner. "In fact, you look as happy as I've ever seen you. Have some more hotdish."

"You make the best hotdish," I said sincerely. Hotdish was some Minnesota thing—and today's, tuna fish and egg noodles with crushed potato chips on top, was particularly sublime.

Abogee was schlooping down his portion, noisily like he did at home, one eye suspiciously on me. I think he thinks if I'm happy, I must be up to no good.

It wasn't always like this. When I was little, I remember adoring Abogee. I used to stay up late just so I could see him when he came home from the store.

"I nyosok chom pwara," look at this little rascally fellow, he'd say to me.

But he wouldn't scold me for being up past my bedtime. He'd make a snack of ramen for both of us. We'd sit there eating while everyone else was asleep.

So, exactly when did Abogee turn so negative on me? When did this "Number one son" thing start to mean I couldn't do anything right?

I tried to make myself glum by thinking thoughts of war, death, destruction, and Spam, but my mind kept going back to the sight of the football turning into a UFO, and a smile tugged at my mouth as if I were a puppet.

At practice the next day I caught a pass and ran an obstacle course of defensemen to bring it in for a touchdown. Coach nodded approvingly.

"You're a twisty little guy," said Kearny, who hardly ever complimented anyone.

After practice I was blabbing nonstop with Mikko, and it felt like my feet didn't bother to touch the ground. At home I said hi to Mrs. Knutson and then to O-Ma, who was getting a lesson in Minnesota cookery. I said hi to Abogee, too, as he sat at the table with a bunch of papers in front of him. He didn't seem to notice I was home.

"Did you have a good time?" O-Ma asked. She was watching Mrs. Knutson add carrots and potatoes to a big pot in which a roast was steaming.

"Yep," I said. I decided that practice had gone so well that I could let the cat out of the bag. "Get this,

I'm trying out for the football team. The team needs a kicker, and with all my soccer skills, I might be able to do it."

"Where were you?" Abogee said.

"At football," I said with surprise. His English couldn't be *that* bad.

"The store should be opening in another week or so. I'll need you to start working there," he said without looking up. His glasses, perched at the top of his head, looked like a pair of sightless eyes.

"Okay," I said, wondering exactly what he was getting at. *"On weekends, like I did back home, right?"*

"After school too."

Oh. I believe Abogee was telling me I couldn't play football. He does this thing where he drops hints, punches in a code, mutates and mutilates words until he can tell me no without having to say no to my face. Occasionally he makes O-Ma do his dirty work, like the time I wanted a mountain bike for my birthday, but mostly he does the job himself, leaving me flapping like a fish pulled up on a dock, trying to figure out exactly what he means.

I let the silence stretch out, thinner and thinner. Tell me no if you mean no, I was thinking. Tell me to my face and give me a chance to argue my point.

"Why don't we wait and see if Chan makes the football *team and then worry about things?"* O-Ma

broke in. *"I think that would make the most sense."*

Abogee looked at O-Ma, kind of surprised, as if the roast itself had started talking.

"Iron River has a wonderful football team. I can't wait to see you play," Mrs. Knutson said as she shoved the roast back in the oven. "I never miss a home game."

Abogee went back to his papers.

After dinner I was doing some push-ups when Young came up to my room.

"How come I never see you at lunch?" She settled cross-legged on the floor.

I told her about the gym, Mikko, and the other football players.

"I didn't know you could do that."

I shrugged. "We're not supposed to, but some kids do anyway."

Young looked mildly shocked at this. She's a big rule follower.

"So, you meeting any cool kids?" I asked, to change the subject.

"It's too early to tell," Young said. "People seem friendly enough, but no one *does* anything around here. I like Donna. She's no SuJin, though."

My knuckles throbbed because I'd been doing the push-ups tae kwon do style on the wooden floor.

"Yeah," I said. "The only guy I've really gotten to

know is Mikko, the one who got me to go out for football."

"I can't believe you're going out for football." Young leaned over to pinch a sore biceps. I tried not to grimace.

"I know you're strong, Oppa, but they grow 'em big up here. Like that one guy who wears the dirty frayed jeans and those T-shirts without the sleeves. He's a monster. There's something odd about him. He smells bad too."

"How do you know how he smells?" He stank something fearsome in the locker room, but then we all did.

"Yuck, Chan, just walking down the hall. He has a cloud around him, you know, like Pigpen in *Peanuts*."

"Can we talk about something else?"

"So what're you going to do if Abogee doesn't let you go out for football?"

My *other* favorite subject, Abogee.

"You think he doesn't want me to go out for football?" I batted my eyes. Young rolled hers.

"Anyone can build muscle, but building brain . . ." she mimicked Abogee's clipped Korean. *"Number one son, you must do something to make this family proud!"*

"Young-ster," I said. "I really do want to go out for football. I mean, I used to think it was a useless sport, but actually I kind of like it."

69

"I know. It shows."

"So what should I do?"

"I'm not sure," she admitted. "Maybe you should ride it out a little first. You know how Abogee is so touchy."

"Touchy isn't the word."

I couldn't help feeling touchy myself. Though I am willing to work hard, I'll never be a rocket scientist. But doesn't talent extend beyond things you do with a pencil in your hand? I worked my butt off to make the soccer team. And while Abogee drove Young all over the freaking state of California for some math tournament, he never came to one single soccer game, even when they were right in the neighborhood.

"Abogee always listens to you, Young," I said. "Can't you come up with some cool argument for football—like studies show that football can help you get better grades, or something like that?"

Young shrugged her thin shoulders.

"I'll try," she said doubtfully.

thirteen

"*Students should now report with their homeroom teachers to the auditorium.*" The principal's voice droned facelessly from the intercom as everyone shuffled out.

We were in alphabetical order, so my seat was right next to Young's.

"Wow, an assembly," she said. "I wonder what's going on."

I shrugged. I wasn't a big assembly type, unless it was quiet enough to allow me to catch up on my *Z*'s.

"Hey, you weeg, scram!" I looked to see ALL-PRO bending menacingly over the kid who had the seat next to me.

"Howdy, pardner," he said, settling in. He looked over at Young. "Who's this?"

"My sister," I said. "Young, this is Mikko."

"You guys are twins? Cool."

"Actually, I'm really thirty-one," Young said. "I flunked a lot."

"Really?" ALL-PRO looked amused all out of proportion to Young's remark.

"Really. Of course we're twins. Can't you tell by the way we look alike?"

Mikko laughed. Young has a long, narrow face and high cheekbones, while my face is as round and formless as a wheel of cheese. About the only thing we have in common is Abogee's cowlick, over the left eye for Young, right eye for me. Mirror images.

"So what is this all about?" I asked.

"You don't know?" ALL-PRO's eyes grew comically wide. "Like, really? It's only the most important event of the school year."

"So why don't you tell us?"

"You wait and see." He winked.

The lights went down and the heavy velvet curtains opened. Behind them was the principal—ALL-PRO's dad—and Coach, and Coach Kearny. The cheerleaders stood behind a table that displayed a row of shining black helmets.

"Ready?" ALL-PRO's teeth almost glowed in the dark.

It couldn't be. The varsity team results were supposed to be announced today—but after school, at practice, I thought.

"Welcome, welcome," boomed ALL-PRO's dad. "Here's the day we've all been waiting for, to find out who will be the representatives of the Miners for the upcoming football season. Let me turn the mike to

Mike—har, har—head coach of the varsity team, Mike Thorson."

As the audience cheered, ALL-PRO whooped like an Indian. Young gave me a look, like who *is* this guy?

Coach took the stage.

"This will be our most exciting season in years," he said, his tan washed out a bit by the strong stage lights. "The last time we went to the state tournament was ten years ago!"

"Bo-ring," whispered Young. "Can you believe we get out of class for this?"

"Shhh." I was engrossed.

"With this year's lineup, we've got a record number of seniors returning, a junior who played varsity last year, lots of talent. This team is *experienced*."

A titter rose from the audience. Ever dignified, Coach ignored it.

"Let's start with the captains. Returning senior quarterback, Leland Farrell."

From the audience, the senior QB climbed onto the stage amid cheers, shook hands with the Ripanen-Thorson-Kearny triumvirate, took a helmet, and stood with it tucked under his arm. The cheerleaders' pompoms made a sound like rain.

Monster Rom Kreeger was the other captain. Young jabbed me with her elbow and whispered "That's Pigpen" when he got called.

"Our junior quarterback, Mikko Ripanen."

"Hmm," said Young. "*He* made the varsity team."

ALL-PRO got out of his seat leisurely and sauntered to the stage. He was all solemn shaking hands with the coaches, but when he was supposed to shake his dad's hand, he reached out and pinched his cheek— to loud roars of approval.

Mr. Ripanen put his hand to his cheek and pretended to swoon.

"People in this school are weird," Young remarked.

More roars, laughter while other names were called.

"And last but not least is our kicker, Jann Kim!"

Jann, Chan—close enough. He could have called me Jennifer, for all I cared.

Young's mouth was open, moving slightly, as if she was saying, "It couldn't possibly be you!"

I floated all the way to the stage. One helmet winked under the lights. I grabbed it. I did my best to look stern, tough, like everyone else in line—but I just smiled like a goon.

fourteen

"And the whole school totally clapped," Young recounted for everyone at dinner. "I had no idea Chan was going to make the *varsity* team."

"It's no small accomplishment, that's for sure," Mrs. Knutson agreed as she poured ketchup on her hamburger. "You should be very proud, young man."

The only one who didn't say anything was . . . guess who. He just muttered darkly to O-Ma about her need to economize, meat like this was expensive. I felt like telling him to quit picking on her.

Is it too much to ask that he be happy for me once in a while? I worked hard for this. On weekends I helped him fix up the store—no small task—and I'd even repaired the leaky sink in the kitchen and fixed up Mrs. Knutson's lawn, which had been well on its way to reverting back to wilderness. But if it doesn't come on a piece of paper, with the grades A through A, he just doesn't give a damn.

Abogee didn't say anything through dinner. Not

even "Pass the rice"—he just reached across O-Ma and grabbed the bowl. Mrs. Knutson politely looked away, just like the first day we sat down to eat together and Abogee belched at the table.

Obviously he was mad. It was a silence you could hear, like when you put a blank tape in the stereo and crank up the volume. The silence just blasts you.

But this time I wasn't going to give in. I wasn't going to panic and say "Okay, Abogee, I'll quit football and work in the store" just because I was afraid he'd sulk.

I knew Abogee was testing me, like in those fairy tales where if I chose the right answer, I'd be rewarded with riches and kingdoms (that is, Abogee not being mad for a while). If not, I'd fall through a trapdoor into a pit of alligators.

The events of the last weeks churned like laundry inside my head. The leaving. My last soccer practice. Saying good-bye to SuJin. The endless ride to get here. Eating lunch alone.

If he didn't have the balls to ask me to quit football *out loud,* I wasn't going to answer, either.

I think he was afraid I would say no, out loud.

"Go out on the slant, long," Mikko said to me, waving his arm toward somewhere out on the field. "Don't turn around until I tell you."

I ran out. The rain-sopped field squished like a sponge beneath my feet.

"Now!" he yelled. I turned. A bomb crunched me right between the numbers.

"Hug it to ya, or you're gonna lose it," Kearny shouted in disgust. "Whatsdamatter, your fingers all greasy from that Chinese food?"

Kearny really yanked my chain sometimes. I think he knew it and enjoyed doing it, too. He was always chewing out people in public, questioning their manhood, trying to get the larger guys to absolutely flatten the smaller ones. It was all part of what he called the "necessary roughness" of becoming a football player. I thought that was bull.

But I wasn't so stupid as to mouth off to him. I knew who controlled the roster for the games.

I had the kicking down pretty well. I could kick at different angles, I could adjust for the wind. I was getting to the point where I could figure out if we needed a straight-ahead boot or a puffy little floater to get through the uprights.

But we all had to play more than one position. Coach thought I should be a running back or a safety, since I was fast. Mikko was trying me out at wide receiver. It was a little frustrating learning the ropes for so many positions, but Coach made it clear that there wasn't room on the team for a guy who just sat on the bench and came out when it was extra-point time. That fancy stuff was for the NFL, he said.

To end practice, after the gauntlet, we had to do a mile run in under nine minutes, which we did. Then we had to do hundred-yard sprints in pads and helmets in under eighteen seconds, which Rom and some of the other bulky linemen *didn't* do, so Coach made us start over from zero. Run. Run. Run till your gut explodes.

The third time, Rom came huffing in at over twenty seconds. I think Leland saw that if Rom hadn't made the sprints yet, he never would. Leland stuck his finger down his throat, hacked up some watery gruel, and the coaches let us stop.

"Let me remind you, gentlemen," said Coach, as we all lay sprawled out like lawn ornaments. Kearny made us get up and move around. "Our first game is next week. Two-a-days start tomorrow. Kindly get your butts to the locker room before six."

"What's two-a-days?" I asked Mikko. "Is it like One-a-Days plus Iron?"

"It is what it is, idiot," ALL-PRO said back. "Get ready for the practice from hell."

fifteen

At five thirty in the morning it is dark. Like opaque dark. I thrashed around for my football stuff, clothes to change into, grabbed my book bag, and headed downstairs.

Abogee was already up. He was sucking down a bowl of ramen. Well, Oodles of Noodles from Northland Foods to be exact. It was perfectly quiet except for that sound, the one that a drain makes right after it's unclogged.

He looked at me a little quizzically, noodles hanging down from his mouth like a mop, but didn't say anything, not even "good morning." *SCH-LOOP!*

"Hi, Pop," I said, not waiting for a reply. I slapped peanut butter and honey together to make four sandwiches. Mikko had turned me on to this combo, which was far tastier than the Spam-plus-mayo, warm and probably salmonella-laden by lunchtime, that Mrs. Knutson seemed to favor. It was nice of her to offer to make our lunches, but Young was always wondering if she was actually trying to kill us off so she could get new tenants. Maybe ones that didn't go *SCH-LOOP, SCH-LOOP* in the wee hours of the morning.

I was out the door by five forty-five. The back of my teeth felt a little fuzzy—I'd forgotten to brush them. No big deal. In football, a certain amount of seasoning is required.

The air was heavy with moisture, which clung like pollen around the pale illumination of the street lamps. There was absolutely no sound except for the slight breathing noise the early morning makes. Perfect. The library was dark, like it was sleeping. I blew out clouds of breath and began jogging toward the school, not because I was late, but because I was feeling frisky.

I cut across the field by the school. Dew slobbered water all over my shoes. The sky had turned from frying-pan black to gunmetal gray. Another day.

Rom was the only one in the locker room when I arrived. This was the first time I had seen him without Jimmi Beargrease attached to his side.

"Hey, Rom," I said as I sat down to change into my cleats. He didn't look up. He was sitting there in his practice shirt, pants half hitched up over the hugest, hairiest thighs I'd ever seen.

Young was right. He did stink. It was the putrefying smell of someone who eats a lot of meat: digested gristle, muscle, veins, and melted fat.

"What are you?" he said, his voice flatter than the EKG of a dead person.

"What?"

He poked me as if he were testing a package of ground beef. "I said, what are you? A chink or a jap?"

Whoa. This guy was my teammate. Or was supposed to be.

"You have a very eloquent way of putting things," I said. "I'm neither Chinese nor Japanese. I was born in Korea."

I finished with my cleats, threw on my practice T-shirt. It crackled slightly, with salt.

"And what are you?" I asked, still trying to figure out exactly what he was getting at.

Rom growled. He reached over and poked me again. "Huh. I'm one hundred percent American, nigger—and don't you forget it."

Holy cow. This guy was calling me chink, jap, *and* nigger. I didn't realize I was so many things to him.

The locker room door opened and a couple of guys shuffled in.

"Hey, Chan. Hey, Rom."

I felt a slight chill in the breeze they'd let in, and then I realized I'd been sweating.

Jimmi didn't show up to the morning practice. No one asked where he was, either. He was there in the afternoon, though. When I walked home with Mikko, I asked him about it.

"Oh, Jimmi lives in the Neeshawatin Res," he said. "He's Indian, if you haven't guessed."

"Hi, Mikko," called a blond girl in an IRON RIVER CHEERLEADERS jacket. She licked an ice-cream cone as she eyed ALL-PRO.

Mikko half-waved at her.

"A few of the kids on the res go to school here," he went on. "But it's like almost an hour away. Jimmi can't get in for practice in the morning, but Rom gives him a ride home at night."

"Rom and Jimmi seem like a weird combination," I said. "I mean, especially given Rom's, uh, opinions."

"It is kind of strange," Mikko agreed. "But to each his own, I suppose."

We walked down Iron Mining Way. Mikko lived on Taconite Avenue, where all the nice houses in town were.

"You live in that big house by the library, don't you, Chanster?"

"Uh-huh." Someday Mikko was going to find out we only rented the top floor of Mrs. Knutson's house, but I didn't want to tell him right now.

Tackling drills. Kearny would toss a ball to the runner, and the defensives went for the tackle.

Catch the friggin' ball, I goaded myself. Mikko had

given me some gloves with sticky fingers, kind of like the Korean grocer ones, and they helped.

"Hup," said Kearny in a bored voice as he sent the ball into a lazy spiral. All eyes were on me as I moved out to get it.

"Down you go, jap boy," hissed Jimmi, cutting me off at the knees and grinding my head into the ground.

Then, under cover of his back, he punched me, in the soft underbelly place where the pads don't cover.

I saw green. The contents of my stomach rose upward, clamoring to become puke. *"Gak."* I swallowed it. It burned the back of my throat.

"Kim, get up, you pansy," Kearny yelled. "Toughen up."

I forced myself to stand, hawked up some phlegm, and spat. There was dirt in my mouth guard.

Damn if I wasn't going to kill Jimmi when the positions were reversed.

"Hup!" Jimmi ran out. I charged. His waist felt like a tree. It was like bringing down a water buffalo. One-two. I did it.

"Jeez-us—what's that you're doing, a dance?" Kearny sneered. "I thought *I* was going to be your date on Saturday."

Jimmi snickered.

This was just one drill, one practice, I told myself.

The coaches told us to hit the showers, and I went

with Mikko to do a few laps around the track. He always did extra after practice. ALL-PRO always went two hundred percent. I admire that in a guy.

Today we had a great view of the girls' tennis team. Every so often, since the courts were next to the field, they ended up whopping their balls over the fence and had to come and pick them up.

"Who's that?" I motioned to a girl whose hair was even blacker than Young's and mine, and was so thick she had it tied on the top and bottom.

"Rainey Scarponi," said Mikko. "Her dad owns Scarponi Sausages."

I tried not to make it look like I was staring at her, but gads, she was beautiful: long legs, muscular arms, and that hair. I must have a thing for girls with messy hair.

"Put your eyes back in their sockets, would ya?" ALL-PRO gibed, punching me in the arm.

We ran, not talking anymore. At one point Mikko gave me a goofy, smirky smile, and I found myself grinning back, for absolutely no reason at all. We still didn't say anything to each other. In the fading light our shadows made one shadow.

sixteen

"*I joined the band,*" Young announced at dinner. "*I get free flute lessons fourth period.*"

"*Chotta,*" said O-Ma, looking slightly relieved. As we had suspected, there were no Juilliard graduates teaching flute in Iron River.

"*And also, we play all the* football *games, so I'll get to watch Oppa.*"

All eyes turned to Abogee.

His face actually softened the tiniest bit, the way wax softens when you warm it in your hand. He loved to watch Young play her flute and never missed a recital, come hell, high water, or earthquakes. So if she was getting an opportunity to play, even in a dorky school band, he would be grateful. And it would be due, at least somewhat, to my playing football—right? And we'd be doing something together.

When we were toddlers, O-Ma told us once, Abogee could not get enough of Young and me, the way we played together, the way we went waddling around hand in hand. *"Your father used to sit for hours watching you two play,"* she said. *"Chan, you used to pat Young's cheeks with your chubby little hand. It would make us all laugh—and want to cry a little bit too. It was so sweet."*

"Field goal practice, team one kicks," Kearny yelled. Coach stood at the side, as he usually did, observing everything like a hawk.

I was the kicker for team one. Jimmi kicked team two. We lined up in formation.

I waited for the snap.

A second later I was flat on my back, staring up at the sky, sparks of light swimming before my eyes. Stars of pain pulsed from my back, shoulders, legs, and head. Rom stood over me grinning, the way I think a poisonous snake would just after it bites someone.

"Buck up there, Kim," yelled Kearny. Coach frowned.

"And Beargrease, close that hole, would ya! Man! If someone doesn't come straight at you, look around. Kreeger, don't use your head to block the ball—even though we know it's your least important part."

I'd been set up. I was sure of it. Rom wasn't that fast; no way he could reach me with that amount of momentum if I had half-decent coverage. Which Jimmi Beargrease was supposed to provide.

This was going to get interesting.

I stayed after practice again. While Mikko jogged, I worked on shortening my kicking time, which was already short. The shadows lengthened, and it was harder to see.

"Ready to go in, buddy?" Mikko asked.

"Yeah. But hey, could you work on some plays with me tomorrow?"

Mikko grinned. He had a gap in his teeth that made him look like a farmboy, like that was where he would put his piece of hay, or his corncob pipe.

"You really work it."

"You were the one who recruited me. I can't let you down."

We headed to the locker room. I limped, not necessarily because my leg hurt, but because everything hurt. I laughed at the horizontal red line the helmet left on Mikko's forehead, although I probably had the same one.

A bevy of girl tennis players fluttered by. The lead girl stopped to say hi to Mikko, so the whole crowd of them stopped too. By awesome luck of the draw, I found myself face-to-face with Rainey Scarponi.

She had a huge racquet case slung over her shoulder. It looked like it could—or did—contain a machine gun. She was looking sort of curiously at me.

"Hi," she said.

Now was my chance. I had to say something. Something good. Something that would get me noticed. I stole a glance at her and saw that she was smiling slightly.

"Duh . . . hi," I said, suave as hell. I studied my shoes. Think of something cool, I ordered myself.

You look like you could be in an ad for something clean—no, that was ridiculous. Brain . . . hello, brain?

"Are the football players going to be at the party?" I heard the other girl say to ALL-PRO. He grunted something unintelligible and then turned to me and said, "Come on, Chan."

He waited until we were in the showers.

"You gotta be smooth, boy," he said. "You can't show you're too interested, know what I mean?"

"Yeah, thanks, Dear Abby," I said. I realized I had totally blown it. I promised to be more surly next time.

seventeen

Even when I was in math class, I ran plays in my head, studied the playbook. When I played soccer, Manuel drilled us over and over, so when you got the ball in a pass at a particular angle, with your opponent leaning over to take it away, your body knew to feint left, dribble, and pass without even consulting your brain. I wanted football to be that automatic for me.

Our next game was away. I must have been one of the few players who liked away games. I got a kick out of seeing the other schools in the area, even if we did have to drive three, four hours to get to, say, Croquette, a town that had a paper mill and smelled like rotten eggs.

Today we were invading Moose Creek. All I knew about it was that it had a mental hospital and a detox center, so referring to someone as having gone "up the creek" was shorthand for a lot of things.

"Look, Chan, bullet hole." ALL-PRO pointed at a

globular swelling in the glass in the door to the school. "But the glass doesn't shatter because there's chicken wire in it, see?"

The wire looked like a bunch of stop signs stuck together, or an M. C. Escher drawing. The glass at I.R.H.S. was nice and clear. For some reason no one had thought to shoot at it.

The locker room was all concrete, covered in lumpy lime-green paint that looked like it had been poured on the walls straight from the can. The rubber mats on the floor were curled and moldy. I'm not that picky, but no way was I going to let my bare feet touch that crud.

"These dudes won the conference title last year," ALL-PRO said. "We were in the running at sectionals, but they just stomped us."

"Do we have a chance this year?" I unpacked my soccer shoes and football cleats. Lately I'd taken to putting the soccer shoe on my right foot when I kicked.

Mikko shrugged. "A couple of their really good players graduated. And we still have Rom and Leland. This year's the one for us if it's any year at all."

"Kim, you're going in," Coach yelled.

We had taken an early lead and were feeling pretty good.

The plan was to fake a bootleg. The wide receiver and I, at halfback, would go out as decoys. Leland would then hand the ball off to Jimmi in a reverse.

Moose Creek didn't bite. A Mack-truck-size guy hit Jimmi, and the ball squirted out of his hands. The ball skittered downfield and I dove for it, ending up at the bottom of a very heavy pile.

Coach told me to come back out.

"You might have to punt soon. Don't want you getting messed up."

"Nice going, Geronimo!" snarled Kearny as Jimmi woozily returned to the sidelines.

"C'mon, Coach. No one could get hit like that and *not* fumble." He was holding his elbow.

"Would you like a little cheese with your whine?" Kearny played an imaginary violin. He always came on too strong, like anchovy pizza.

By the half we were tied.

"We can do it," Coach said. "We just have to make that extra push."

"Look," said Kearny. "If we push 'em back now, we'll just breeze right down to State. We'll be golden. So go out there and finish 'em!"

I didn't have a real idea of how important a team Moose Creek was to beat, until we lost.

We lost by only one point—they made a freak two-point conversion—so I didn't think it was so bad.

But there was a deadly silence in the locker room, as if a glass jar had descended and sucked all the air out. No one talked. Hell, no one even breathed.

Then Coach spoke.

"You've made this all the harder on yourselves," he said. His voice seemed to be coming from another dimension. "We want to go to State just as much as you do, but Coach Kearny and I can't do it for you. We'll have another crack at them at sectionals, but it's going to be an uphill battle."

"Lousy, lousy defense," Kearny snarled. "The line, except for Kreeger, was an absolute sieve. My ninety-year-old toothless grandma could've run past you guys. You aren't men, just a bunch of pussy-boys."

"We screwed up" was all that ALL-PRO said to me on the bus ride home.

eighteen

ALL-PRO was out sick, so after practice I worked on my kicks and did a few laps until the sun went down. The girls' tennis team must have had a meet, because the courts were empty.

The locker room was deathly quiet, although it smelled like a passel of steaming, putrid guys had trooped through, which, in fact, they had. Added to that was the smell of the stuff the janitors used to clean the showers—some major fungicide, I suppose. It was acrid and burned my nose.

I shed my pads like I was a snake molting, and peeled off my T-shirt and pants. The concrete floor was littered with torn tape and used Band-Aids. One of them was a Sesame Street Band-Aid—Bert and Ernie. It made me grin momentarily, but I was still tired. I sat down.

Even if I had been expecting it, I don't know what I would have done.

A rough, mildewed towel suddenly covered my

face—my nose, eyes, everything—and a split second later bodies leaped on top of me, grabbing my arms and legs. Whoever they were, they were strong.

I kicked out, hit something, and heard a muffled "Damn!" But someone still had my arms and I couldn't twist away.

Arms grabbed my legs, and I felt my jock strap being pulled down. I tried to kick, but I couldn't move. Then I realized they were tying my ankles with my jockstrap.

I hate the thought of being tied up. It makes me sick. Everything in my insides jumped and skittered like tiny fish. I twisted, kicked with both feet, yelled, and got a mouthful of towel for my trouble.

"A little necessary roughness, huh?" It came out barely audible, like the hiss of a tape player. There were at least three of them, I think. They got my hands tied.

Someone shoved me into the lockers and I fell like a stone to the wet floor. I couldn't breathe. I twisted my neck until a bit of the towel gave by my mouth. I gasped in the air.

I screamed. The cold cement pressed into my hip. "Come back here, you cowards!"

I was tied with some kind of cloth; once I wriggled my hands free I saw it was one of my socks. There was blood staining it. The jock was still knotted tight around my ankles—one of which was beginning to swell, right above the bone. Now that I'd stopped yelling, I realized it hurt like hell. It was golf-ball size now, which meant it would be much bigger later.

"Who did this?" I yelled. No one answered. Only the lockers stood in silent, solemn testimony to what had happened to me.

nineteen

"What happened to your leg, Oppa?" said Young when I limped through the door. I felt like I was going to puke.

"I wiped out on the street walking home," I said, doing my best to control the shakes in my voice. "I think I sprained my ankle. Ha, ha."

"Did you hit your head, too?" she said, pushing aside my hair. "Ewww, this looks terrible."

"Actually, I fell in the locker room—but don't tell O-Ma. She thinks football is dangerous."

"Let me get you some ice. You should have called. Someone could've picked you up."

But then I would've had to explain why I was crying.

I felt like I'd been raped, honestly. Being tied up and left naked on a dirty locker room floor is probably the closest you can get to it.

It hadn't been horseplay. People wrestled and did dumb stuff in the locker room, sometimes with a couple guys ganging up on another. But this was different.

It was all I could do to keep myself from breaking down again.

It had to be the guys I knew. Who else would have access to the building at that hour? Who else would know I was there?

My teammates.

"What happened to you?" said Kearny when he saw me limp into the locker room, my ankle huge with swelling and an Ace bandage.

"I fell in the locker room," I said, looking around. If anyone was going to have a crisis of conscience, it would be now.

No one did. At least, not that I could see. Rom was sitting on the bench, adjusting his pads. Jimmi sneered.

He had a bruise on his nose.

"Nice going, klutz," he said, when he saw me looking.

"You're not going to be any good for the team this week. We got a game Friday, you know. Jesus." Kearny was talking as if he thought I had done it on purpose.

"I'll come to practice and watch," I said.

"What's up, Jann?" Coach walked in. He bent down and gave my ankle a squeeze. I barely swallowed a scream.

"How'd you do this?"

I repeated my story.

"Did Doc Larson take a look at it?"

I shook my head.

While everyone practiced, I went to see the team doctor. He sat me on the training table and opened up a tackle box that contained all sorts of gauze and cotton nose plugs and bandages and clips for the pads.

"Looks like a bad sprain," he said. My ankle looked like a ripening mango; it was about that color, too.

"I heal fast."

"I think you'd better have it x-rayed. There might be a fracture."

My heart stopped.

"I'll give you a lift to the hospital right now."

"Is it going to cost money?"

"Did it happen out on the field?"

"In the locker room."

"Close enough. No charge for players, professional courtesy and all that." He reached over and pushed the hair on my forehead, the way Young did. "And where did you get this?"

"Same place."

He gave me a look, like I must be the most accident-prone dope he'd ever met. How could someone who hurt himself like this ever manage to pull himself together to be a football player? I stubbornly kept my mouth shut.

"Get a tetanus shot while you're at it," he said. "Come on. My car's out back."

I hated it, sitting in the X-ray room, waiting for the pictures to be developed.

A little necessary roughness, huh? I'd heard that voice before, for sure.

What was going to happen if there was a fracture? I'd be out for the season like Gary, the other kicker. That would be it. That would be the end of my so-called football career.

"Got a little roughed up on the field?" The radiologist came in with the X rays in hand. Even though he was wearing these professor-type glasses, he looked like he was twelve.

"I guess." My fingers started nervously playing with each other. Was this guy being so cheerful because he had good news—or was he being cheerful because he was preparing me for bad news? Or was he just practicing his bedside manner?

He cleared his throat and shuffled the film, rattling my nerves at the same time.

"Your ankle's not broken," he said. "We just need to fit you with an air cast. But we're still talking two–three weeks of rehab before you go back to play."

I wanted to kiss him.

"And you're going to have to be careful in the future."

"I will, I will," I said, practically hopping off the table. Let the Iron River Mafia try to get me again. It doesn't take a whole lot of guts to gang up on one bone-tired guy. If they wanted me to give up and die, that was going to be the very reason for me to keep on going. I was one tough L.A. mo-fo.

I hated sitting out the next game. While everyone else suited up, I wore my civvies and sat on the far end of the bench reserved for guys like Otto Jensen, a special-ed kid who was on the team but never played.

Every time we scored a touchdown, I got up, ready to get in the field for an extra point. Then I'd sit down, embarrassed, glad only Otto was there to see my mistake.

Jimmi went in as kicker. He made one extra point, failed another. His punt got returned for a touchdown.

There is a God, I was thinking. We still won.

twenty

In shop we were doing woodworking, which was kind of cool.

Shop was required for boys, home ec for girls. Next year we could take automotive repair as an elective, but I knew Abogee was going to make me fill up that space with calculus instead.

Young, on the other hand, wanted to give up her home ec class to take calculus now.

"Home ec is so stupid," she told me. "And the trig class bores me to tears."

Mr. Ripanen said no way, however.

"He had the nerve to say I'd probably appreciate the home ec classes after I was married. And he called me *young lady*."

"Maybe he couldn't resist the pun," I said.

"People around here aren't subtle enough to pun."

"They're not very pun-ny, eh?"

"Shut up, Chan."

✳   ✳   ✳

Me, I enjoyed the easier classes. I loved being able to get all my homework done in study hall and still have enough time to flip a paper football around with Mikko. I don't think people at Iron River are necessarily dumb, they're just not that uptight about school.

Some of the kids at El Caldero, a magnet school, were just too intense about studying. The Korean kids were the worst.

"Jae Moon's dad said that if he got into Harvard, he'd get a BMW," my friend Andy told me once as we watched Jae lug home a wheelbarrel's worth of books.

"So if his abogee can afford to buy him a BMW, why doesn't he send him to private school?"

"Don't know. Maybe he can't because he's too busy saving up for the car."

I had cut out a football shape from a flat piece of wood. I'd planed it, stained it, painted on the stripes and laces. Now I was using this electric pen that would burn lines right into the wood for the finishing touch.

MIKKO • ALL-PRO • RIPANEN I wrote in the middle of the plaque, squeezing in the last letters. When it stopped smoking, I handed it to him.

"Why, that thing is bee-yootiful, Chan!" ALL-PRO grinned. "I need to glue something on the back so I can hang it on my wall."

"Mr. Munchie," he called to our teacher, "do you have those little mounting hooks?"

Mr. Munchie paused, looked at my work. I beamed proudly back at him.

"That's not exactly what I had in mind, Chan," he said, smoothing his mustache. "I was hoping you'd make something more realistic."

ALL-PRO was working on a bear. A few of the other guys were doing fish.

"You mean that's *not* a real football?" ALL-PRO gasped.

"It looks like something you'd buy at the state fair," Mr. Munchie said, walking away. I didn't know if it was good or bad, but I assumed the worst. I wasn't worried, though. Abogee wouldn't go ballistic over a poor grade in shop.

"Only the classiest state fair," I told Mikko.

After we won our next home game, the talk was that we were all going to go to some big party.

ALL-PRO and I went to the parking lot for our ride. Rom was waiting, at the wheel of a pickup truck.

"We're not going to the party in *that*," I said to Mikko.

But he'd already vaulted into the back with some of the other guys.

They sat expectantly, like a bunch of migrant farm-workers, which reminded me of L.A.

Almost every day the Mexicans would wait in a crowd in front of the Extravaganza, with their rakes and shovels and whatnot. It looked like there was going to be a rumble or a revolution. But no, a guy or a lady would drive up in a Beemer, and another would follow in a pickup. The Beemer person would lean out and go you, you, you, and you, pointing with a finger, and the guys would hop in the back of the pickup to be taken to the rich person's house for a full day of farm or yard work. The others would wait until other people showed up, or if they didn't, they would go home to wait for another day.

Manuel did this for a time, he'd told me. He hated those rich people. *Los pinches ricos,* he called them.

"What'cho lookin' at?" Rom growled, gunning the engine.

"C'mon, Chan, let's go," said Mikko.

"Yah, okay." I jumped in. I was picking up some weird Swedish accent from these guys. Next thing you know, I'd be yodeling.

Rom drove about a hundred miles an hour over an unpaved country road, making those of us in the back bounce around like a bunch of beets. I grabbed the side of the truck and hung on.

The truck skidded off the road.

"Duck," said ALL-PRO, pushing on my head.

Two seconds later, I heard noises like bones crackling. Leaves were falling all around us like pieces of paper.

I think we were running straight into a line of trees. What a stupid way to die, I was thinking.

Then everything stopped. I looked up. The night was jet-black. No light, not even pinpricks of stars.

I made sure my teeth were intact.

"Damn," I couldn't help saying. "Where are we?"

"We're at Rushmore, an abandoned mine pit." Mikko's voice. "Come on this way."

A mine pit? I wondered as I followed his voice. Leaves, brush, and stones moved underfoot.

Suddenly there was light. Warm orange light from a bonfire burning at the center of a huge crater. This place really was a pit, surrounded by walls of rock and a ring of trees. Now we could all see each other in the fire's glow.

"Glad you guys finally got here," said one of the girls, a cheerleader. She still had her short skirt on. It made me feel cold just looking at it.

Most of the guys rushed the beer. I edged toward the fire, trying not to shiver.

"You're lucky we're having this Indian summer," ALL-PRO remarked. "Some years it snows in September, and you'd be freezing your little L.A. butt right off."

Indian summer? This wasn't exactly what I'd call loincloth weather. I'd been getting plenty frosty in practice, especially in the morning when there was no chance of the sun providing any warmth. Otto, the special-ed kid, had started wearing thermals under his uniform. But he was the only one.

It didn't take me too long to determine that Rainey Scarponi was there with a bunch of girls from the tennis team. I'd have known where Rainey was anywhere. I wanted to go up to her and talk to her—but right now that seemed about as conceivable as flapping my arms and flying off to the moon. I turned to ALL-PRO.

"How's Gary doing?" I asked. I didn't really care, but I sort of felt obligated to ask. After all, if not for him, I wouldn't be on the team.

"I'm sure he misses us." Mikko walked over to the keg, which was sunk into the ground. He grabbed two cups and filled them up.

"I don't miss him a whole lot, though," he continued. "He's a total weeg, always inciting Rom and Jimmi into all sorts of stuff. That kind of person is bad for the team." He handed one beer to me. "I like having you around better."

I didn't know what to say to this, except "Thanks." I took a sip of my beer, but I didn't suck it down. I'm not all that crazy about the taste of it, to tell you the truth.

"Does Rainey Scarponi have a boyfriend?" I asked, trying to sound casual.

Mikko laughed. "You still got your eye on her? I don't think she's seeing anybody. She doesn't go out with a lot of guys. Don't exactly know why—she's a pretty girl. But then again, Rom and Jimmi and Gary really got on her case last year—to give you an example of their weeginess."

"Like how?"

"They started calling her 'the sausage queen'—you know how her dad owns Scarponi Sausages. But this was totally out of the blue, just to be mean."

"What a bunch of knobs." I was beginning to believe more and more that Rom and Jimmi had to have had a hand in what was done to me. I would have suspected that Gary guy, too, except he was home with two broken legs.

"It got pretty bad. At homecoming they had this sign out on the field before the game. It said 'Rainey Scarponi, Bohunk Sausage Queen.' "

"Did they get suspended, or what?"

Mikko shrugged. "No one could prove they did it."

"What?" I said, feeling outrage for this girl I'd hardly talked to.

Mikko shrugged again. "We probably should've done something about it. But do you know anyone who can hold a line better than Rom?"

"No." I didn't. No one came close.

"Come on," Mikko said. "Let's go talk to her."

✳   ✳   ✳

Rainey Scarponi had blue eyes. Bluer than blue, behind long, dark lashes that knocked me out. She didn't look exactly excited to see us. She smiled kind of stiffly.

"Hey, Rainey," Mikko said. He sounded a little stiff himself. "Have you met Chan? He's the new guy from L.A."

"Not formally," she said. "Hi, Chan."

"Hi, Rainey." Rainey, Rainey, Rainey. It was like I'd heard that name before, but I know I'd never known anyone named that. Maybe I'd dreamed about her, maybe it was one of those predestination/past-lives kind of crap, who knows? I already felt protective of her, like I'd kill anyone who ever tried to hurt her.

But the problem was, I couldn't think of a single thing to say—again. The waves in my brain had gone dead and flat as Christmas decorations after Christmas. I'd blame all the times my brain had bounced around in my helmet for this, but it somehow only happened when I was trying to talk to her.

"So, do you miss L.A.?" she asked. I paused, opened my mouth—and then all this stuff just came bubbling out. I turned into a blab-o-matic, talking on and on about how the air in L.A. was so dry that we had a cactus on our lawn, how we used to play soccer in a garbage-strewn park, how I missed going to the beach. I guess "Do you miss L.A.?" was a question I'd been dying to answer, but no one had bothered to ask until now.

Mikko had gone somewhere. Rainey and I kept talking.

The autumn moon, which had been caught in the high branches of the trees, pulled clear. It was so bright, it looked like a disk stamped out of new copper. I felt like sitting down and writing a poem rhyming "moon" with "Rainey," but first I wanted to keep talking to her, for about another hundred years.

There was a touch on my elbow. My heart nearly stopped beating.

"Hey, Chan." An unexpectedly deep voice behind me. ALL-PRO. "Sorry to break up the party, but Leland's going back into town. Didn't you say you needed to get back in before eleven?"

I checked my watch. It was ten forty-five.

Abogee and O-Ma would be coming back from the store around eleven thirty.

Here I was, on a moonlit night, with a girl with awesome black hair. I was close enough to kiss her. I could have kissed her. Well, I'm pretty sure I had the guts to do it. But now it was too late. I had to go.

I wanted to kill myself.

twenty-one

Opening day. I had been at Froggie's since eight in the morning polishing, stacking, mopping—you name it. I ran hot water through the Slurpee machine and the most amazing iridescent colors came out.

Young came in too. She doesn't like to do a lot of heavy lifting because she's afraid for her hands, so she did the dusting and kept me company.

I had to stock the magazine rack and found— much to Abogee's surprise—that Bong had sold some porno magazines when he ran the place. The magazine jobber had come by and given us the exact same inventory Bong had used, and that included *Playboy* and *Penthouse* and this magazine called *Jugs* that was lying between *Family Circle* and *Popular Mechanics*. I don't know if it was Bong or the franchise, but that incident was the closest thing I'd ever seen to Abogee saying something bad about his brother.

Abogee's one of those people who's religious but doesn't go to church. He would if he had the time, I suppose. He called the distributor up and called him all sorts of names in Korean, including "devil." Not only that, he wanted the guy to bring his truck back right that minute and take away the "filth." It really wasn't the guy's fault, since Bong had ordered the magazines in the first place, but I think Abogee probably blamed the guy as a corrupting influence on Bong.

Anyway, I preferred our old store to this one. At the Extravaganza, no one told us where to put the beef jerky, exactly how much soap you needed to clean the floor. And we didn't have those god-awful contraptions like that thing Young and I dubbed the "hot-dog Ferris wheel": a circular cage containing a dozen hot dogs slowly rotating under glass, sweating in the beam of a hot light.

But the biggest drag by far was the uniforms: paper hats and aprons that said FROGGIE'S EXPRESS on them. The hats were the pits because they had two cutout eyes that were supposed to look like the top of a frog's head, but the model they'd used was obviously a toad, and these distinctions were important to me.

Not to mention that it made you look completely and totally asinine. As much as a hard, smooth football helmet makes you look tough and scary, this thing made you look like the world's biggest weeg.

Abogee wouldn't bend on the hat, though. I was wearing that hideous thing even as I wiped counters by my lonesome. The only way I could get by was if I made sure to never, ever glance into the anti-shoplifting mirror at the register.

A fair number of people came in that day to check out the store, and everyone bought something, at least a quart of milk or some bread. Young and I worked until seven thirty; then O-Ma came in to take over.

Finally we were making money.

twenty-two

"I dare you," Young said, holding out a greenish-yellow orb. Green Apple Killer Sour Death Ball.

Another thrilling Saturday at Froggie's.

"Simultaneous death balls," I suggested. "First to pucker loses."

"You're on." She handed me one, unwrapped another. "Ready, set, go!"

Killer Sour Death Balls are the latest thing in mouth torture since Zots and Pop Rocks, those things that were like eating Alka-Seltzer. Chili KSDBs are red and cinnamon hot. The green ones are sourer than a thousand lemons.

The saliva flowed. The walls of my cheeks closed in as my mouth practically turned itself inside out. So did Young's.

"We need more practice," she said.

"Hey, man," said a youngish guy in a John Deere cap, as he walked up to us at the counter. "You got any of those Satan cigarettes?"

"Excuse me?" I said. Young looked horrified.

"You know, Satan. That's a brand of cigarettes."

"There are not, to my knowledge, any cigarettes that go by the brand name Satan," I said.

The guy's pants were covered in a bright-red dust. He had an IRON RIVER ORE PLANT hard hat in one hand. The name written on it in marker pen was Borgstrom. Mrs. Knutson said the mining companies had set up the trust that had built and now maintained the high school. It seemed weird that kids went to a school that looked like a mansion and then ended up working in the dust of the mines, after.

"You used to carry them when that other guy ran the store," he said, doing an earnest search of the rack. "There they are!"

"Where?" I said with disbelief. I couldn't believe Abogee would let something like that in the store. He practically had a fit when he saw the Underwood Deviled Ham label, thinking there was a canned devil inside it or something.

"There . . . over there . . ." he said, urgently pointing. "Right under the Salems."

I looked. There was a brand of ladies' cigarettes in a pastel box. You got a free pair of earrings or panty hose or something once you amassed a black-lung's worth of UPCs. The cigarettes were called Satin cigarettes.

"Um," I said gently, as if I was breaking the news

that he was being held back in second grade for the third time. "Those are *Satin* cigarettes—you know, like satin sheets. For the ladies."

"Uh . . . huh." He nodded slowly, as if he didn't quite believe me. But the package was purple and pink, for goodness' sakes.

"Gimme the Marlboros then."

I got a pack down.

"You guys don't have any of that huh-huh stuff, do ya?" he said suddenly.

Huh-huh stuff? Was he talking some weird Iron River language? Young and I looked at each other and shrugged.

The guy looked disgusted, unsatisfied. He spun on his heel and left, leaving the coins he used to pay still spinning on the counter.

No one else came in for a while, so Young and I restocked the shelves, careful to follow all the franchise instructions, which I thought were stupid. What would it matter if the Spam was placed above the Spaghetti-Os? Mrs. Knutson would certainly approve of such a product placement, but who else would care?

"Do you think Abogee still has his gun?" Young said out of the blue. Back in L.A. we'd known a number of people who'd been robbed, even killed, so Abogee had bought a gun.

"I wouldn't be surprised," I said. "Did I ever tell you how the store got held up?"

Young looked shocked. "What? No, never."

"It happened when I was twelve. O-Ma had to go somewhere, so Abogee had me at the store in case he needed some help.

"He had to go into the basement for something and told me to man the register."

I remembered that day so clearly, the way the store smelled, vaguely fruity like chewed gum. How I'd almost hoped we'd get a customer so I could test my skills on the cash register.

"These three guys came in," I said. "They didn't say anything, they just stood at the counter. I was about to ask them what they wanted, but then I saw the gun."

"Jesus, Chan." Young hardly ever, ever swears. She put a hand to her mouth.

The gun had been a dull color, fitting snugly in the man's squat fingers. Guns definitely looked cooler in the movies.

"I figured I knew what they wanted, didn't need to wait for them to tell me. I gave them everything, even the food stamps."

"Oh my God. Where was Abogee in all this?"

"Downstairs, luckily. Could you imagine what would have happened if he'd busted the whole thing up with his gun? The store is not the best place for a shootout."

The robbers had been calm—cold—almost polite. They stashed the cash and the gun and walked out, as if they'd merely been in to get a bag of Bar-B-Q potato chips.

"And then Abogee came up a few minutes later, and I told him what happened."

"So how come you never told us?"

"Well, Abogee didn't tell the police because he said they wouldn't do anything and you can't trust them. We didn't tell you because we didn't want to scare you. It wasn't like Abogee said 'Don't tell Young and O-Ma.' It just turned out that way."

And even now, I wasn't telling Young everything.

After the robbers left I sort of went into shock.

Abogee came up and found me sitting in front of the till, its drawers open and empty. I was sure he was going to lose it, now that the drama was past.

What'd you do? How much money did we lose? Why didn't you call me?

But no.

He didn't even ask what happened.

He just looked at me, gently patted at my clothes as if he was checking for bullet holes or missing limbs. His mouth was turned down, like he was on the verge of crying. He almost looked like a little kid who'd lost his favorite stuffed animal. When he found nothing missing or perforated, he grabbed me and held me close, like he hadn't done since I was really, really small.

117

He smelled like garlic, oily hair, and sweat. I wished he'd never stop hugging me.

"Anybody ho-o-o-me? This place has lousy service!"

Young and I went to check the voice out. Mikko was standing at the register. I saw him look at Young and smile.

"May I help you, sir?" I asked.

"Yes, could you ring these up?" he said. He picked up two bottles of Gatorade and a quart of milk.

"Anything else?" I asked, quite the professional as I rang up his stuff. He shook his head. For fun, I threw a Green Apple KSDB into the bag. Maybe in the future he could participate in the KSDB Olympics with us.

"See ya later." He winked at Young. She blushed. "Chanster, I'll catch you at the park, right?" We were going over there to practice some—just us.

"Yah."

I meant to put thirty cents for the KSDB into the register, but Young and I became absorbed in straightening the Astro-Pop display on the counter. Astro-Pops were shaped like rockets, in three patriotic colors: red, white, and blue. We arranged them so they stuck out in different directions, looking like they were going to blast off all over the store. Very eye-catching.

A lobster claw grabbed my arm.

"Don't you be passing off free things to your friends," Abogee hissed.

It took me a second to realize what he was talking about.

"It was a thirty-cent piece of candy, Abogee," I said. My fist clenched underneath the counter. *"And I was planning to pay for it."*

"Don't you use your smart mouth with me. I am your father."

"I'm not being smart, I'm telling you the truth." You just never listen, I was thinking.

"You, you—" He raised his hand. In that split second I decided if he was going to hit me—just as he'd probably been wanting to for years—I would absolutely let him.

"Oh, hi." Mikko materialized in front of us, like on *Star Trek.* Abogee's hand dropped. "Gosh, I'm sorry, I just totally spaced out and forgot to pay for this." He laid three shiny dimes on the counter and smiled winningly at Abogee.

"Sorry again. See ya."

Abogee skulked back downstairs. I dropped the three dimes—*ping! ping! ping!*—into the till.

"How'd he know?" Young said with awe. "Does he understand Korean or something?"

"No, he just understands the universal language of the way uptight jerkface father."

"Chan!"

"It's true," I said heatedly. "He never gives me—or anyone—a chance. Then he goes around acting so righteous like he's Mr. Perfect or something. Need I remind you that we are here on account of some screwup of his brother's? But no—Bong's fine, and I never do anything right."

"Chan, don't talk like that." I could tell I'd upset her.

"Okay, I won't," I said slowly. "But that doesn't change anything."

When my shift was over, Abogee came by. It looked like he was going to say something—I have no idea what—but then he stopped. I took off my hat, laid it on the counter, and didn't say a word either. Then I walked out the door of the store and kept on going, alone.

twenty-three

In school, banners started appearing in the halls. RIVER-FEST HOMECOMING! I guess the big thing was who was going to be voted king and queen.

Leland Farrell, our quarterback, was one of the candidates. I imagined Mikko would be there next year too. The thing of interest to *me* was the game.

Every so often at the home games, I kind of wished Abogee and O-Ma were there to see me play. I mean, everyone else's parents were. Mikko's dad cheered so much at the last one that his voice was all hoarse over the intercom the following Monday. I would like to think that Abogee's attitude toward football would change if he'd sit down and actually watch a game.

But I didn't know that for sure. At least I had Young sitting in the band rooting for me, and Mrs. Knutson hollering from the front row.

The day of the game, I could barely sit through class. After freezing through two-a-days and watching game tapes all week, I just wanted to get out on the field.

At dinner Mrs. Knutson talked about how exciting the game was going to be, perhaps not realizing that that was a subject best not discussed when Abogee was around, as he was tonight.

Young left the house with me. The band people had to get there early to antifreeze their instruments. It was going to be a cold night.

"Be careful walking in the dark," O-Ma said to us. Abogee stood behind her, like a shadow, and watched us go.

Everyone has his own pregame ritual. Leland sits in the shower in the dark and makes funny humming noises like *Ommmmmm, Ommmmmm.* Mikko listens to *Mad About Mozart* on his Walkman and won't talk to anyone. Jimmi won't shut up. Rom paces the floor like a zoo animal that's going to start biting at the bars of its cage any minute.

Me, I do what I did before soccer games: breathe really slow, meditate a little, and think about what I might be able to do in the game.

Coach walked into the room, bringing us back into the here and now.

"Listen up," he said. "You know the drill. Little

Moon has a loose offense but an excellent defense. So linemen, you push open the holes. We really have to drive through. Defense, you have to hold that line. The guy to watch is their running back, Jukich, number seventeen. He is fast. And remember—the whole town's watching and counting on you. Don't let them down."

Vaguely, outside, we could hear the first strains of our school song.

"Let's go." Coach put his hand out. We all crowded around him, touched hands, and yelled *"Miners!"* before we exploded out the door, into the lights.

The ref handed the football and tee to me.

I love the kickoff. It's my little moment of glory. Tonight even the breeze seemed to be waiting as I dug in my cleats.

The line charged with me as I ran. I booted and kept going. Full steam. Coach said he liked the way I attacked everything I did. Kicked off but still ran for—and sometimes made—the tackle.

The evening sky turned from a dark pale blue (a color hard to explain if you haven't seen it) to bruise purple. It didn't take us long to get the ball back.

The coaches called for the streak-and-curl play. The running back ran straight up the flat into the end zone, curled back, and snagged Leland's pass, dipping back into the end zone for the touchdown. The band cranked out a fight song. Coach motioned me to go out.

I blasted the ball, practically before the Little Moon Pirates even moved. The ball went end over end, right through the uprights.

Whee! There was a shrill noise, like the cry of a strange bird. Strange, yet familiar. It was Young's flute. She was blasting a C note in celebration.

When we were on defense, the coaches kept calling the blitz because Rom could run right through and nail the quarterback. On third down Rom sacked him. The poor slob was taken off the field on a stretcher.

Kearny patted Rom's butt and handed him a skull decal for his helmet, where he already had two. Rom slapped it on right away and beat his chest.

"Get back in there," said Coach. "Nickel zone."

Coach sent me in as strong safety. I was so pumped, I could feel a pulse beating in my neck as I ran onto the field.

"Down, set . . ." The Pirates handed off and bodies collided.

The running back was heading right into my zone.

He had the ball.

He came up on me like a freight train, arms pumping like pistons. I leaped after him. His knees knocked me in the jaw, but I held on with everything I had. His curses were like music.

We held them.

"Nice job, Kim." Coach patted my back. "Beautiful tackle."

"You're a tough little bastard," added Kearny. I glowed, my face steaming in the frosty air.

At the end of the third quarter we were ahead, 14–6. On fourth down at the Pirates' twenty, the coaches decided to go for a field goal.

Mikko caught the snap.

I was just following through the kick when I saw the green of a Pirate's uniform rushing at me. How'd he get through?

I heard a crunching noise, and then I hit the ground.

I was going to tell that Pirate knob to get off me, but then I realized I had no voice. And that I couldn't breathe.

I'm not sure how Coach knew I was in distress, but he ran onto the field.

"Can you get your helmet off, Jann?" He touched my arm gently, like you might a baby. He took out my mouth guard.

I wanted to breathe. But something hurt really badly, really sharply, like someone was zapping me in the side with an electric cattle prod.

"Medical!" He yelled for Larson. "Can you breathe?"

The magic question. I shook my head. Sledgehammers were starting to pound my temples.

"Okay, Chan." Larson's voice. "Try to sit up a little if you can."

I straightened. There was a burning, sticking feeling in my side. I doubled back over.

"It might be a rib," Doc Larson said to Coach. "Chan, try to sit up as much as you can. Breathe in slowly."

My breath started coming back in short little spasms. It was like being in the ocean when waves keep knocking at you. I needed more air. I gulped. Jerked. Wheezed. I sounded like a cow with emphysema.

Whatever was wrong with my ribs, I was glad to be able to breathe again. I'd just gotten the wind knocked out of me, that's all it was. When Coach asked me to stand up, I did. Cheers flowed down from the stands, and I saw from the scoreboard I'd still made the field goal. I wondered if the guy who hit me was going to get a skull.

Doc Larson took me to the hospital, where an X ray revealed I had bruised my ribs but not cracked any of them. He said I was still good to go. Lucky. He wound some gauzy junk around my torso and told me not to let my girlfriend hug me too hard. I was psyched I'd still be able to go to the dance.

I had the doc drop me off at the high school so I

could take half a shower. The guys all cheered when I showed up in the locker room. They were all lying around in a sea of pads and stinks and smiles, so I knew we'd won.

"Glad you're okay, Jann," said Coach. "As I was saying, while we're that much closer to State, it gets harder from here, not easier. Everyone's going to challenge us for the title, so we've got to do what we've been doing, and double it."

"We're going to have a conditioning workout tomorrow at eight," said Kearny. "So go home early and get some sleep."

"Uh-huh," said Leland. He gave us a look, like yeah, right.

"The coaches totally kicked Beargrease's butt," Mikko informed me later. "The Pirate guy got a roughing penalty, but the coaches aren't letting Jimmi play blocker anymore because he can't contain."

"Whatever," I said. At this point I was believing more that Jimmi didn't cut the mustard than that he was letting people in to gish me.

"Gotta pull your weight around here," ALL-PRO declared as he opened a new three-pack of Fruit of the Looms.

"New undies, huh?" sniped Leland. "Some cocky weegie thinks he's gonna see some action tonight."

"That's for me to know and you to find out," said Mikko with a sly grin. "Maybe I just ran out of clean ones."

"Who're you going with?"

"Cindy Gray."

"Oh, that girl, she'll do it with anyone," said Rom from the other side of the room. "I mean, even more than the rest of the cheerleaders. Believe me, I know."

"Kreeger, you are so full of it," Mikko said. "No girl would want to touch your hairy butt."

Mikko patted some Brut onto his face. I wished I had enough whiskers to shave.

"You and your ribs ready to go, buddy?" He put his hand up for a high-five.

Slap!

I was ready.

The school dance reminded me of one of those After School Specials on television. There were streamers all around the gym, punch in a bowl, and chaperones. Corny to the max. Maybe dances at my old school were like this, but no one I knew had ever gone to one.

Corny or not, it was worth it to see Rainey in a slinky black dress with blue trim that exactly matched her eyes. Man, it was worth it.

Mikko dragged me into the bathroom first. He'd brought some booze in trial-size shampoo bottles. We stood in the large handicapped stall and downed them. The bottles still tasted of soap.

"I think it was a mistake to bring Cindy," he said miserably. "Now she thinks I like her, when all I wanted to do was come to the dance."

"You don't like her?" I said. Now I could distinguish between all the blond cheerleaders: she was the one with the interesting ice-cream-cone eating technique.

"She's just too, too—um, enthusiastic."

"So what are you going to do? Stay in the bathroom all night?"

Mikko wrapped an arm around my neck. It felt as heavy as an anaconda. "You're a cool cruiser, Chan. My whole life has changed because of you."

He was getting drunk. I took the bottle away, pretending to drink it myself. If I sneezed, I expected bubbles of Pert to come blipping out.

"Come on. Let's go dance this stuff off."

Rainey was an awesome dancer. I was merely okay. For all my soccer and tae kwon do prowess, I couldn't quite get my feet to do what I wanted them to do when out on the dance floor. I liked it when they played slow songs, because I got to hold her, and I didn't have to move around as much.

"Look who's with the sausage queen!" said Rom, just loud enough for us to hear. He was with one of the cheerleaders with the big boobs.

"Get a life," I said, pulling Rainey closer. Sometimes, if you get happy enough, even total butt-wipes don't bug you.

"He is the worst kind of person," Rainey whispered to me. "Dumb and with muscles."

"Don't forget evil," I said. She laughed, felt looser in my arms. I loved everything about this girl—her teeth, her heavy lashes that gave her a sleepy, dreamy look, her hair . . .

"How come we didn't go to your house for pictures?" she asked. Apparently for Riverfest, the whole tradition was to go to everyone's houses and manufacture Kodak Moments in four different living rooms. We only did three.

My excuse was going to be that O-Ma and Abogee were both working at the store, which they probably were. But somehow the words wouldn't come out.

"Do you not want your parents to meet me?"

I sighed. It's not always convenient to date intelligent, perceptive girls.

"Uh." I rifled through a list of other possible coverups. Then I gave up. Lying can be a lot of trouble.

"Only two things might bother them. You're not Korean, and you're a girl."

"Oh," she said.

"My parents don't want me to date until I get to college, and then it's got to be a Korean girl."

"Oh." She looked disappointed.

"You'll meet them someday," I told her, pulling her a little closer, even though a fast song had begun. "We just don't always see eye to eye on stuff, especially me and my dad. All I can do is ask you to be patient, I guess."

"I understand," she said.

We ended up dancing more and more into the shadows away from the center of the dance floor. I pushed my head toward hers in the dark. She was exactly the right height. I heard the sea in my ears.

It's strange how life moves in fits and starts. During the first day at school, minutes passed agonizingly slowly. Now, as we kissed, time was a bullet train hurtling through the black of a tunnel.

twenty-four

The coaches had decided to start watching our weekly game tapes at ALL-PRO's house. Before, we'd watched them in the cold and damp of the gym, crammed in front of the grainy screen provided by the AV department. The Ripanens' basement was a big improvement, fully carpeted with a complete home-entertainment center and a billion comfy seats.

There is something excruciating about watching yourself on video. The first time I saw myself on film, it was like, who's *that*? What I saw onscreen was some doofus galoomping gracelessly up to the ball and hacking at it. It couldn't have been me—except he was wearing my number, 22. Later, I saw the same guy fumble a ball, in a manner worthy of *America's Funniest Home Videos*.

To put it mildly, it was torture being forced to sit through endless slo-mos. About the only good thing was that the guys didn't rag on you, because soon enough the coaches would point to something *they* did wrong. The video eye sees everything.

We settled comfortably in front of a wide-screen TV. Next to it someone had made a bookshelf. I admired the woodwork, definitely A+ shopwork. In the other corner was a home gym, situated so that you could watch TV or listen to music while you worked out. No wonder ALL-PRO was all-pro.

Kearny popped in the tape of our last game with Moose Creek and yelled at us for a while. Then the homemade tape footage fuzzed out, giving way to real TV sports. Channel Five, state tournament, Moose Creek versus Elko Center. Coach Kearny fast-forwarded through the commercials and pregame show.

The players collided on the screen. They bashed into each other like angry rams. They tackled, blocked, punched, gouged, and scored. We began to push and shove each other off the couches.

This showing was more than a strategy session, I was realizing. If we managed to beat Moose Creek, that would be *us* down there at the Humphrey Dome, on TV. Talk about motivation.

Then the coaches left. Rom dug out the videos he'd picked up at one of the video stores. Iron River, which had no bookstore, had three video stores.

"So did you get a football movie or something?" asked Mikko.

"Naw," said Rom, looking sidewise at me. "I got us some kung-phooey movies."

I raised an eyebrow.

"Jean-Pierre Vandervanter. He's good."

Leave it to Rom to know exactly how to work my nerves. At my tae kwon do *dojang*, a bunch of us had practically formed a club of guys who hated those white-guy martial-arts movies. We were sure we could beat any of their butts in a *real* fight. Jean-Pierre especially annoyed me because he went around claiming to be some kickboxing champion, but no one had ever seen him fight outside of a movie set.

I knew I was going to hate this one when it opened with weird *boing-boing* Asian music.

The plot of the movie was this: Jean-Pierre's brother had been brutally tortured and murdered by some incredibly ugly Chinese martial artists. So J.P. goes to China to avenge him. He meets this beautiful Chinese woman (a girl, really) whose father is about a thousand years old and happens to be the martial-arts monk at the Shaolin Temple. She, for her part, does things like walk on J.P.'s back to help him with his "training."

J.P. beats all the Chinese guys, no problem, using all the tae kwon do moves—tornado kicks, somersault kicks—showy stuff you'd never use in a real fight. He earns the undying gratitude of the lotus blossom and her family because those evil guys were also the bandits who had terrorized their village for years.

Wouldn't you know it, but Rom had not one but two of those movies. The next one was *Kickboxer in Korea*, for God's sake. Of course the Korean guy is an ugly stupid mo-fo who wears a Korean flag on top of his head—upside down, I might add—and he tries to throw J.P.'s concentration off by doing things like kidnapping and raping J.P.'s new (Korean) girlfriend. I'd never seen a Korean guy who had a Chuckie-the-killer-doll smile or a brow thick enough to park a car on, unless it was in the Museum of Natural History.

"Kill! Kill the chink!" Rom yelled, as the Chuckie-smiling "Korean" guy threw some powder in J.P.'s face to make him blind. "Can't trust those lousy chinks—they cheat! You're way better than him. Kill him!"

Chinks. Uh-huh.

My guts tightened. The room seemed to grow very, very still.

Rom snuck a look at me as if to say, "What are you going to do about it, huh?"

A few of the guys shifted in their seats. Even Mikko looked like he didn't know what to do.

The movie kept on going. Jean-Pierre kept pummeling the Asian baddies, who were coming out of the woodwork, all buckteeth and slit eyes, straight from central casting.

"Buncha chinks," Rom growled at the screen.

"Shut *up!*" I yelled, jumping to my feet. Everyone looked at me.

"Geez, I'm just joking," Rom said innocently. "What are you getting so uptight for? It isn't like I'm calling *you* a name. I'm doing it to the guys on-screen."

"Yeah, like hell."

"You calling me a liar?"

"You calling Rom a liar?" Jimmi echoed.

"You don't know crap about martial arts," I said.

"Oh, yah, and you do?"

"Koreans invented tae kwon do, which is the stuff Jean-Pierre is doing."

Rom laughed.

"Okay, so how come there are no Korean martial-arts heroes? Who's the Korean Jean-Pierre? Or Dolphin Lundegaard? Or Stephen Segull?"

"They're all fakes!" I yelled.

There was some kind of pressure building inside me. I wanted to quit arguing with Rom and just kill him.

"Yah," Rom said lazily. There was a knowing gleam in his eye. "Like fer sure, if a bunch of guys jumped you, you could kill 'em, huh?"

My mind leaped back to the raunchy taste of the towel shoved in my mouth. The guys jumping out of nowhere.

"A little necessary roughness, huh?"

I ran over to the pile of scrap lumber by the

bookshelf and grabbed a few of the leftover boards. They were pine, sanded. Perfect.

"Scrap?" I said to Mikko. He just stared at me.

"You don't need these, right?" I turned my voice up. He nodded uncertainly.

"Okay, here, Rom, Jimmi, come up here and prove your manhood," I said, thrusting the boards toward them. "Hold these and I'll show you what I can do."

"Whoa, you're messed up." Jimmi took a step back.

"You have no idea, asshole. Come on. Take them."

"Chan . . ." said Mikko, now that he saw what I was intending to do. "Don't let these guys get to you. Look, we're in the middle of the season. If you hurt yourself—"

"I know what I'm doing!"

But did I? A large knot in the grain could stop me. If Jimmi or Rom moved the boards at the last second, I'd be dead. The skinny bones connecting the knuckles to the wrist would split like twigs. I'd seen it happen before. But all I wanted to do was break those boards, as if I'd be breaking Rom's head at the same time.

Jimmi was starting to look relieved.

"I knew you were chicken," he said.

I looked at the two of them standing there holding the boards.

When you dive off a high board, the square of

water below looks so small, impossibly small. Just like when you hit a board, it looks hard, impossibly hard.

Crack! A horrible, terrible, splintery sound. Raw pain shot through my hand, up my arm.

The boards fell to the floor.

"Oh geez," breathed Jimmi.

"Wow," said Leland. "If only you could do that in a game."

Rom just laughed.

Everyone wanted me to show how I did it, but I went home soon after that. I somehow felt dirty, like I'd flashed everyone on a dare or something. I didn't feel the way I thought I would. Mikko didn't say much to me either. He seemed kind of disappointed in me.

twenty-five

I think the store must have been doing halfway decent, because Abogee hired a night manager, Greg, so that Froggie's 24-Hour Express could start living up to its full name. Before, we were closing at midnight.

O-Ma also declared that she would take Young and me to the mall in Little Moon Bay so we could get real jackets, now that the temperature was only in the forties and fifties during the day. I said I'd wait for my letter jacket, which, the coaches said, we juniors would get early this year so we could wear them to the state tournament. God willing.

"Okay, guys, the F-S dinner is going to be this Saturday," Coach announced as we all luxuriated in the stink and steam of the postpractice locker room. Rom's newest ritual was to stop taking showers a whole week before a game so his pads—and his hide—radiated the most lethal smells. Poison gas. He smelled worse than the bums who used to come into our store for quarts of malt liquor.

"We're doing the dinner a little earlier this year so you juniors can get your letter jackets. Also, because we want you to spend a little quality time with your old men before we concentrate on practice. It will be this Saturday at the VFW, seven thirty. That means coats and ties, for the uninitiated."

"Letter jackets—sweet!" someone said.

"What's F-S?" I said to Mikko.

"Father-son," he said. "You bring your dad."

Father-son. For the wildest of moments, I imagined I'd ask Abogee to come to the dinner with me, and he'd say, "Son, I'd be proud to. When is it?"

But then I realized that was only an episode of the sitcom in my head, *The Lovingly Wacky Kim Family*, which had absolutely no bearing on reality. For starters, Abogee would never call me "son." And could you imagine what he'd be like at a football dinner? Especially with dads like Mikko's around? Abogee would probably go around spouting his favorite antifootball sayings.

"Anyone can build muscle, but building brain is more difficult."

"Football is so popular in this country because it provides people with an excuse to drink beer."

"In Korea, grown men would not waste their time fighting each other over a tiny ball."

Uh-uh.

"Coach, I don't think my dad can make it. He has some stuff to do at the store that day."

Coach looked at me.

"Maybe Mikko's dad can adopt me for the night," I suggested.

"Your father owns Froggie's, right?"

I nodded.

"That must be a lot of work."

"Uh-huh. Sure is."

"Well, tell him I hope he can come. But if not, I'm sure Rip would love to have another son."

Chan Ripanen. For a second, I couldn't help thinking how nice that sounded.

When I asked ALL-PRO if I could go to dinner with him and his dad, he said sure, but he gave me a bit of a funny look.

"Too bad your dad's going to be busy."

"Yeah. The store takes up a lot of his time."

"Looks like it. Looks like you and your sister help out a lot too."

"I guess so."

Okay, I felt a little guilty about dismissing Abogee without even asking him. But it was more like I was doing it for him, doing my usual job of trying to figure out what would best please him—or at least preserve the uneasy peace between us—without actually telling him what was going on.

*   *   *

I was doing some extra-credit reading for English when Abogee emerged from the trapdoor like a jack-in-the-box.

"How is football?" he said, hoisting himself into my room and sitting down on the floor.

I was stunned by two things: He was speaking English, and he was voluntarily uttering the word *football.*

"It's okay," I said, as naturally as I could.

"I meet Coach, that man, Do-Sun."

"Coach?"

"Yes-u. He come into store today."

"Uh-huh."

"So this man, Do-Sun, say you good at football."

I sat up in a hurry. Not at the news that Coach thought I was a good player—which was thrilling in itself—but something else really threw me.

Abogee actually sounded a little proud of me.

I had a weird sensation. It was one of those feelings where, for the fleetingest of moments, you think everything's going to be all right. Like everything, even between me and Abogee.

"So did Coach tell you about the father-son dinner Saturday?"

Abogee nodded. "I will go," he said.

I was just about to tell him how happy I was that

he was coming, when he said, "This man also be you and sister calculus teacher next year."

Oh.

"Maybe we should bring Young along, so we can butter him up at the same time." I knew my sarcasm would be lost on him.

"So I have Gary work Saturday evening," Abogee said. He got up stiffly, his joints crackling and popping like mine did during morning practice. He disappeared down the stairs, and the door sprang shut behind him.

I shook my head to clear it before settling back down to the books. I would be bringing Abogee to the father-son dinner. How about that.

twenty-six

"What are we expected to wear to this dinner?" Abogee said to me. He actually sounded a bit bewildered. I'd already told him nice clothes, but I guess that wasn't enough.

"A tie," I said. *"Nice white shirt, pants."*

Abogee dug into his drawer and dug out a heinous turquoise-and-yellow clip-on bow tie, which looked like a butterfly poised for flight.

"No, a real tie, like this." I pointed to the classy red-silk number that Young had bought me last year for my—our—birthday.

Abogee sighed, but dug out the one tie he owned, the one he wore to weddings and funerals back in L.A. He knotted it first, then slipped it over his head like a noose. I noticed that his neck no longer filled out his shirt collar, so the tie hung a little low, like a necklace.

Abogee also seemed to have grown more white hairs since we'd been here. His hair, raven-black, showed the little white shoots really plainly to the eye. Still, when I stepped back and looked at him in his coat, tie, and pants (shoes would come later), I was struck, as I was from time to time, at how good-looking he was. Tough, sort of like a Korean Clint Eastwood. He probably doesn't know this, but I hope my face will look craggy like that, after I get older and some of this baby fat melts away.

I'd never been inside the VFW before. It was a brick building squatting by the side of the highway with a big sign: VETERANS OF FOREIGN WARS. In front it flew the American flag, the VFW one, and a huge black POW/MIA flag. On Saturday nights the place filled up for bingo and country/western dances. On weekdays you might see old guys in flannel shirts limping into it. ALL-PRO said that the guys at the VFW, along with the Elks and Rotary clubs, were the ones who raised the money for our new Riddell helmets.

Tonight there were plenty of cars in the lot. I recognized the Hunchback—Leland's banged-up Omni hatchback—Rom's red pickup, Kearny's sporty Firebird. Abogee parked Lou next to the Hunchback and actually made the Hunchback look good.

We made our way past the bar and TV lounge into a hall filled with tables covered with white paper. Name tags in swirly writing told us where to sit.

Everyone looked scrubbed and presentable—

almost too presentable. I was used to hanging out with everyone stinking, retching, and burping, looking imposing in helmets and pads and ground-in dirt. Now everyone looked smaller, more like kids and less like warriors. It was vaguely disappointing.

Abogee studied the walls, which contained murals: furious orange, red, and green scenes of battle, painted comics style. I took him to our places and checked out the tags next to us. We were going to be sitting next to ALL-PRO and his dad.

"What's this?" said ALL-PRO, looking at the other tags. "Romulus Kreeger? Jimmi Joseph Beargrease?" He looked like he was considering moving them, but then he turned to Abogee.

"Hi, Mr. Kim." He held out his hand. "Mikko Ripanen. Remember me?"

Abogee's smile was a little stiff, as if he needed more practice to get it right. Still, he took ALL-PRO's hand.

Across the room, Coach and ALL-PRO's dad were rolling in some shared laughter, Coach bent over double, slapping his thigh, ALL-PRO's dad going "Haw-haw-HAW!" like I'd never heard him. The two of them had played on the Miners together, twenty-four years ago.

When we sat down to eat, Jimmi hadn't shown up yet, but Rom had. His father introduced himself as *Dr.* Kreeger. He wore a nice three-piece suit and a ring with a diamond in it. Abogee seemed impressed.

Then he turned around and asked me in Korean where the bathroom was.

"That was a beautiful twenty-yard pass you completed last week," Dr. Kreeger told ALL-PRO.

"Dad, shut up. The coaches are about to speak," said Rom.

My mouth popped open like a mailbox, but no one else at the table—including Dr. Kreeger—seemed shocked.

Dinner was mud-colored roast beef, mashed potatoes and gravy, corn. Abogee ate carefully, sawing each little piece of meat just so. My meat had been tough and gristly, and I left a bunch of chewed wads on my plate, but Abogee ate everything. For dessert we had Jell-O with pink foamy stuff on top.

As coffee was being served, the coaches started circulating from table to table. Dr. Kreeger got up and started saying hi to people at other tables. I just sat there with Abogee, both of us silent.

"Hi, Mr. Kim, glad you could make it," said Coach. "Jann has worked really hard this year. We're very proud of him."

"Oh, my son terrible," Abogee said, the briefest of smiles betraying him. Korean parents *always* counter a compliment to their child with an insult, to appear properly modest. "Chan, he lazy, not study. No good at football either."

Coach looked from Abogee to me, as if he was trying to get a clue on how to take it. I thought for a second of letting him think that Abogee was mean, but I grinned back at him instead. He seemed a bit relieved.

"Jann's not only talented, but he's also a hard worker," Coach went on. "I've never seen a kicker work so hard to get downfield."

Abogee just nodded. I don't think he could tell downfield from a shuffleboard court.

"Hey, Mikey!" Coach went on to talk to Mikko's dad. "Oh, geez," I heard Mr. Ripanen say. Soon the two of them were guffawing again, Mr. Ripanen clapping his hand on Mikko's shoulder. They were talking about when the Miners went down to State—back when *they* were in high school. I guess Mr. Ripanen had caught the winning pass. The way the three of them were laughing, it was like they shared a secret language or something.

"Okay, quiet please." Coach was at a podium set up in the front of the room.

You could have heard a piece of mooshy roast drop to the floor. A good coach is like that—he commands attention the minute he walks into a room. And he makes you want to do things for him not because he yells at you or shames you, but because you want to make him proud.

"It's always great to be at the father-son dinner, to have the dads sharing in some of their boys' accomplishments. This year we're really on a roll. Of course, we're not there yet, but our record up until now is something to be proud of. It just goes to show that if you work together, you can achieve anything.

"So in a show of faith, we have some awards for you hardworking juniors. We're going to count on you to grow up, provide the leadership for the underclassmen next year."

The coaches started handing out different awards. Mikko got "Best Arm for a Junior," and when he went up, the coaches presented him with a black-and-red letter jacket. I almost gasped, it was so beautiful. The sleeves were thick black leather, the body heavy red wool with a big IR on the front.

"This next one is the 'Twinkle Toes' award for our guy Jann, who comes out and kicks and then runs like hell to make the tackle. He's not just twinkle toes for his magical kicking, either: He's a real wiry runner, an excellent back. Greased lightning. This one's for you, Kim."

The applause picked me up by my armpits and escorted me to the front of the room. I came back with my prize—it felt like it weighed thirty pounds—and I couldn't help looking at Abogee and grinning, a little. Abogee looked back at me and nodded. There is a drop of pride inside that Abogee statue somewhere, I think.

149

"We gotta get Thorson to quit calling you Jann," ALL-PRO said, already wearing his new jacket. "It's driving me crazy."

"Did you have a good time, Abogee?" I asked as we got up to leave.

"Interesting," he conceded.

On the way out we passed a mural I hadn't seen before. A guy was running out of the jungle, firing guns in both hands, Rambo-like. There were faceless enemy soldiers in the background, but I noticed that they were colored in yellow paint. Hmm.

And Rom and Dr. Kreeger were looking at it.

"My brother died in 'Nam. Khe San," I heard Dr. Kreeger mutter as we passed them. "Damn gooks."

"Dad, I've heard you tell that story a billion times. Don't make it a billion and one, okay?"

Abogee looked over at them, not because of what they'd said, necessarily, but because of the tone in which they'd said it. I stepped behind them and opened the door for my father, which is what all good Korean boys do.

twenty-seven

"I want to see what eating in the gym is like," Young announced as she, ALL-PRO, and I made our way to school in ALL-PRO's new Ford Probe. The ink had barely dried on his driver's license.

"It's nothing very exciting," I said. "It's just a place to hang out."

"Why don't you come and see for yourself?" ALL-PRO turned a bit from the wheel to look at Young, who was sitting in front.

"Really?" she said, with a little squeal that was new to her. I hoped she wasn't picking up any weird Iron River speech patterns. "Can I bring Donna?"

"Sure, whatever," he said.

I had this semi-strange feeling that Mikko liked Young, and vice versa. I mean, at first I wasn't sure— I was just picking up circumstantial evidence. For instance, Mikko seemed to insist more and more that we meet at *my* house, and when we did, he seemed to always have an ear out for signs of Young. And

Young always came home with this weird hopeful/expectant look on her face.

It was semi-strange, not fully strange, because it was ALL-PRO. If it were any other guy, especially someone on the football team, I'd want to kill him. I mean, I am Young's oppa, after all, and it's my job to look out for her. And to me, there's hardly a guy that exists that's good enough for her. Especially not the guys in the locker room, who seem to think you handle a girl the same way you handle a football.

"There are two of you?" said Rom, at lunch. Today he was wearing a shirt that said TEN REASONS WHY A BEER IS BETTER THAN A WOMAN.

"She's my sister," I said as menacingly as I could.

I think for the first time I noticed that Young is really pretty. I mean *really* pretty. Even among all these blond buxom beauties around here. Young is just unique, with her straight glossy hair and awesome bone structure. I was glad all of a sudden that she dressed on the frumpy side and hung out with quiet, smart girls like Donna. Could you imagine what life would be like if I had to be pulling jerks like Rom and Jimmi off her all the time?

Young and Donna sat in the corner and ate together, like chipmunks. To my relief the rest of the guys ignored them.

"Thanks, Oppa," Young said as we walked back to

our lockers together afterward. "I just wanted to see how the other half lives."

"Don't thank me. Mikko was the one who invited you."

"Yeah, but he did it because he's your friend." She hugged her books to her chest. "It's wild, Oppa. I was just writing a letter to SuJin telling her how you've become this popular football star."

"Popular? Dream on."

"Of course you're popular. I've heard girls talking about you."

"About me? What'd they say?"

Young laughed, sort of pushed me away.

"Your head is swelling as we speak."

"No it's not. Come on. Tell me."

"I just hear them talk, about how this football player or that is so cute. And your name comes up under the 'cute' category. Girls say Rainey is really lucky. That's all I'm going to say."

"Are you joining us tomorrow, dear sister?"

"No thanks. This was fun for a day, but, uh, football players don't have the daintiest eating habits."

"I guess," I said. I was wondering if she was referring to Rom's chewing with his mouth open, Jimmi's rasty fat-crusted baloney sandwiches, or Leland's dumb "see food" seafood jokes. Even ALL-PRO was a sight, trying to eat four or five pb&h sandwiches in the allotted time limit.

Well, we were football players. What did she expect?

Our season ended early because it got cold sooner up north. If we won the Moose Creek game, it would be almost a month—and more freezing practices—while we waited for the southern conferences to catch up, and then we'd all meet at the heated Humphrey Dome in the Cities around Thanksgiving.

I'd been writing to Manuel, telling him he'd have to come visit, try the cold out for himself.

One morning Young and I stared out the window together.

"Wow," I said. "Where'd the green go?" Our lawn looked like silver Christmas tinsel. We high-fived each other.

"Frost," Young diagnosed. "This is only the beginning. Just think, Oppa, we're going to have our first snow! I can't wait."

On the way to practice that morning, the tops of puddles were layered with brittle ice. But Mikko kept saying over and over again that this weather was strangely warm; by this time they almost always had snow.

At practices we froze for the first half hour, especially if the wind was blowing. It was painful. Then we'd be dripping sweat, which didn't feel so healthy either. But the coaches told us we had to buck up, so we did. Coach wore a big fat IRON RIVER FOOTBALL parka, but Kearny toughed it out in just a tiny windbreaker, to show us he was with us.

In school my grades were okay, but I was glad they'd be coming out *after* the state tournament. You could say I was a little distracted.

My first thought when I got up was football.

After the morning practice I was half asleep all day.

When I woke up at three, it was time to do it all over again.

After that I just wanted to soak in Mrs. Knutson's tub. Sometimes Young would sit outside the door talking or playing me a new song she'd learned.

Tonight I came home ready to ease myself into the tub, but then I stopped. What was that delicious smell?

Korean hamburgers! Wow! I immediately volunteered to set the table.

We sat down to Mrs. K. and O-Ma's version of hamburgers—beef patties coated in egg, soy sauce, and green onion and cooked in sesame oil.

"I had to use this other *kangchang*, Chungking soy sauce, and corn oil for sesame oil," O-Ma apologized. I was already inhaling about three burgers. A layer of kimchi on top and real rice, not Uncle Ben's, would've made it perfect. But then, you can't have everything.

"The last time I had Chungking was at Donna's house," Young said as we gobbled, earnest as pigs at a trough.

"Her mother had bought all this chow-mein stuff and used the recipe off the can," she continued. "And then when I came in the house and went 'Yum, what *is* this?' everyone just looked at me, like I was supposed to say 'Ooh, chow-mein medley is my absolute favorite dish!' It didn't even look anything like the chow mein at Fortune's Garden."

"Yeah," I said. "Like when I ate over at my friend, uh, Ron's house"—only Young knew Ron was actually Rainey—"her, um, *his,* dad was trying to explain to me how a ravioli was like a wonton, not realizing that I am the Chef Boyardee king: cheese ravioli, mini ravioli, roller coasters—I stock them all."

"Not to mention that ravioli is closer to *mandu* for us, not wonton. Geez."

"Gosh," said Mrs. K. "I learn so much about Korean culture from you two."

Abogee glanced up at O-Ma. "The taste of this is good," he said, chewing noisily.

Young and I had finally convinced Abogee that eating loudly—a compliment to the cook in Korean households—was considered rude here, but Mrs. Knutson was busy eating a second helping, and O-Ma looked happy.

"Chan, it's so exciting to see the town rooting for

you young people. All those GO MINERS! signs all over town," Mrs. Knutson said. "Gosh, if you won, you'd probably get your picture in the paper, and my, you look so handsome in your letter jacket."

I nearly blushed. Mrs. Knutson had recently told Young and me that she and her husband had had only one child, a girl, who had died in a boating accident when she was five. Mrs. K. kept saying how nice it was, with our arrival, to have "children" in the house again.

"I was reading in the paper how people buy GO MINERS! merchandise in certain stores," O-Ma said, a thoughtful, concentrating look coming over her eyes.

"Oh, you mean the boosters pins?" Mrs. Knutson said. "Last year they had little mittens, which were much cuter, but the pins are okay. I get mine at Sue's Sweet Shoppe. Would you like me to get you one?"

"I was thinking *we* could sell some at the store, maybe other things."

Abogee sat up at the mention of "the store." Back in L.A., O-Ma had gotten this idea from talking to the customers that the store should carry Drano and Alka-Seltzer (not to be mixed, of course). Abogee deep-sixed it, saying no one goes to a produce store for those things.

O-Ma, however, insisted. I think Abogee ordered the stuff just to prove her wrong. And wouldn't you

157

know it, both Drano and Alka-Seltzer became best-sellers. Lots of people get clogged sinks and clogged guts late at night, when the drugstores and hardware stores have closed.

"What a great idea," Young said. "Like, you know how we already have those Froggie's commuter coffee cups? I bet if we sold Miners T-shirts and coffee cups and stuff like that, people would buy them."

"I know I certainly would," Mrs. K. said. "And I bet my friends from church and the hotdish club would too."

Young and I exchanged looks. Hotdish club?

"In fact," she went on, "an old friend of Ole's"—that was the late Mr. Knutson (God rest his soul)—"runs a novelty printing store. Ooh, maybe he can make those foam hands that say WE'RE NUMBER ONE—I adore those. Let's see what he can do for us in a hurry."

"Oh, yes," O-Ma said, eyes sparkling. "We can donate some of the money we make back to school."

Abogee had stopped eating. He was looking at all of us, sort of bewildered. I did my best to translate, but I'm not sure how well "booster pins" and "novelty printing" came out.

"We should check with franchise first," he said.

O-Ma shook her head. "We ask, they say no. We don't ask, what's the harm? We supporting the school this way."

The doorbell rang. It was ALL-PRO. Mrs. K. let him in, and he sat down at the table as if he'd eaten here a thousand times before.

Except this was the first.

"Hi," he said. His face was scrubbed and beaming.

I introduced him to O-Ma and reintroduced him to Abogee, describing him as the principal's son, the one who gave us a ride to school the one day a week we didn't have morning practices.

"Would you like something to eat?" O-Ma said. "We're having Korean hamburger tonight."

"I just ate a full meal at home," ALL-PRO said. "But how can I resist something that smells this good?"

O-Ma looked just a tad smug as she got up to get him a plate. She bumped into Young, who was exiting the kitchen, already having gotten him one.

"Thanks," he said to her, as if he were a diabetic and she were bringing him insulin.

"Mikko plays football with me," I added. "Quarterback."

"And quite a one," Mrs. K. said. "He played on varsity as a wee sophomore. I remember that game where you carried for over one hundred yards and I don't know how many receptions."

"You have a fan," I told ALL-PRO.

Young and I did the dishes, as we always did, and ALL-PRO helped. Then we watched TV, all of us smooshed on the couch. Young and ALL-PRO sat together, their hips touching.

I kept my eye on them, though. I really did.

I never saw Young look so happy, ever.

Until I saw her wearing ALL-PRO's letter jacket, that is. On her ninety-pound frame, it looked like she was wearing Godzilla's letter jacket.

"Where'd you get that?" I said, trying not to sound overly sarcastic.

"I want to go out with him, like on a date," she said, her jaw set in determination.

"Yeah, right," I said. "*You* tell O-Ma and Abogee that."

Actually, I thought, it would be good if she did. Maybe she could clear the way for Rainey and me to come out in the open. We had started making out in the dark corners at school just because anyplace out of school carried some risk. I'd rather face the wrath (such as it might be) of Mr. Ripanen than of Abogee any day.

"Well, what do you think they'd say?"

I shrugged. "Maybe they'll surprise you. I don't know."

"Think so?" I could tell she really, really wanted to be optimistic.

"You won't know until you try."

Young didn't wear the jacket home. I think she left it in her locker, because when ALL-PRO came to pick us up the next morning, she was wearing her thick down jacket. Meanwhile, he was freezing his patooties off in the same light jacket he'd worn all fall.

"If you get pneumonia before the tournament, Coach is gonna have your head," I advised him.

"Mind your own beeswax, buddy, mind your own," Mikko said. He sounded incredibly cheerful.

"But why not?" Young's voice filtered out the closed door of O-Ma and Abogee's room. *"Everyone else does."*

"College isn't so far away." O-Ma's voice, low and trying to soothe.

"I don't want to wait until college! I want to go on a date *like a normal person in high school."*

"I said no." Abogee's voice, like Darth Vader's. It seemed to slip under the crack of their door. *"You are a good Korean girl. Dating is for Americans and their bad values."*

"I am an American!" Young's voice was getting high, almost voiceless. *"I don't understand why everything American is bad and everything Korean is good. Why did we leave Korea, then?"*

"We came here so that you selfish children could have a better life. And as long as you are in my house, you will do as I say. I don't want to see that Meek-o boy here again."

"But he's Chan's friend too." There were tears thickening her voice.

Abogee said something, squawking, unintelligible.

"Then why don't you just lock us up here, while you're at it, so you can boss us around better?"

I heard a THWAP! and I cringed, but then realized it was the sound of flesh on wood, a table, maybe. Not flesh on flesh. If Abogee ever hit Young . . .

"Go to your room now. I won't have any more of your silliness. I don't understand—you used to be the best child."

I heard movement toward the door, then realized, too late, that I was about to be caught eavesdropping. No way I could sneak back down the stairs fast enough, so I dove into Young's room. Not the smartest thing to do, but the only alternative.

Young appeared, like a ghost, in the narrow room. She didn't look at me, but she must have known I was there. She closed the door softly, too polite to slam it.

"They're so unreasonable!" she moaned, falling like a rag doll onto the bed. I sat down next to her. "All I want to do is go to a movie with Mikko, get a pizza, for God's sake."

Her hair was stuck with tears to her face. I brushed it away. She curled away from me like a shrimp.

"Shhh, shhh," I said, rubbing her back. I couldn't think of any words of comfort; I just felt bad for encouraging her on what had now been revealed to be a suicide mission.

"Oppa, we get good grades, work, all that. Why can't O-Ma and Abogee let us have just the littlest amount of freedom? No one else I know studies as hard as we do, or works at a store. Everyone I know just goofs off. Even Donna sits around watching TV on weekends."

A vein in her temple throbbed.

"I don't know what to say, except sorry," I said. "I guess in hindsight, if Abogee can get so angry about my suggesting we leave an old Buddha statue behind, it was stupid of me to think he'd take dating very easily. Sorry."

"They have no idea what I could do."

I stared at my sister. Do *what*?

"What I mean is that there is so much trouble we could get into, but we don't. So when I want to be an adult, come out in the open about wanting to date, it's like they think I'm some kind of slut or something."

"Well, what do you think's going to happen if they find out about Rainey?"

"It's not the same. You're a boy," Young declared. "Boys can't be sluts."

"Still, I'm not going to let them find out if I can help it. I'll cover for you, too."

"Thanks, Oppa," she said sadly. "But what am I supposed to do? Start sneaking around?"

163

"But Young, promising not to see Mikko is like promising not to breathe. I mean, you'll see him at school, and he's my best buddy."

"I'm sure when he finds out I can't go out, he'll get another girlfriend anyway. All those cheerleaders are always slobbering all over him."

"I don't think so, kid," I said. "Mikko is the kind of guy who sees things through. He's loyal."

She breathed a little, hiccuped.

"Life is so unfair sometimes, Chan."

I knew Young wouldn't sneak around. She just wouldn't. I never felt like *I* was doing anything wrong when I snuck around with SuJin and now with Rainey, but Young had totally different standards.

"One thing I hope you'll think of," I said, "is Mikko's feelings. If you have to let him down, let him down easy."

"Of course, Chan," she said. "Of course I'll think about him. I *love* him."

I stared at her again. My sister was beginning to surprise me in so many ways.

twenty-eight

"They don't have a crazy house there for nothing," Kearny was telling us as we watched footage from Moose Creek's last game: a 36–0 rout of Little Moon. "These folks is nuts—and they get nuttier as the season goes on. Remember last year?"

"Tommy, Leland's older brother, got a concussion," ALL-PRO told me. "This guy speared him in the jaw on a false start—and didn't even get a penalty."

This year, though, I guess we had Rom as our resident nut. He'd been going berserk lately and no one, not even Coach, seemed to be reining him in at all. If anything, they seemed to encourage it.

Last week he'd pulled a drinking fountain out of the wall just to see if he could do it, flooding the hall by the principal's office. But nothing was done, other than to call the janitor.

And then there was the impromptu scrimmage with the JV squad when their game got canceled. Some of the freshmen on that team don't weigh a hundred pounds dripping wet—but Rom ran right through them, as he would a two-hundred-pound tackle. He left one poor center crumpled on the field, crying. The JV coach complained. Kearny dismissed him.

"He's doing you a favor, really. It's necessary roughness. Helps you weed out the kids who aren't tough enough. No crybabies allowed on varsity."

"What, are you nuts?" said the JV coach. "You think this is funny?"

Kearny leaned back and said, coolly, "Do you want to practice with our championship team or not? You decide."

The coach said nothing.

Rom also continued to serve in his capacity as our resident stink bomb. You could always smell him, even in the cold air: decaying fish, old socks, sweat, meat past the expiration date, a gallon of milk left out in the sun.

"You should see him during wrestling season," ALL-PRO commented as I wrinkled my nose when we jogged by him, finishing our laps. "Some of the heavyweight guys practically pass out before the match starts. The word *smegma* mean anything to you?"

I thought I was going to hurl.

"My mom makes me and my sister take a bath whenever we have to go see a doctor," I said.

ALL-PRO's eyes glazed over. Imagining Young in the bath, no doubt. Jesus.

"The point being"—I slapped him—"that if I ever have to see Dr. Kreeger, I'm not going to bother."

"Uh-huh."

twenty-nine

In less than a week, Froggie's had a whole rack of GO MINERS! merchandise: buttons, T-shirts, commuter coffee cups, banners, seat warmers, hats, and, of course, Mrs. Knutson's beloved foam hands. She bought three and gave two away.

O-Ma had placed the stuff strategically by the door of the store. When I worked on Saturday, I saw that a lot of people walked out, saw the display, and then headed back. That meant I had to do twice the math, but I didn't mind, really.

The coaches told us to wear our "dress" jerseys to school on Friday, as if the whole school didn't know we were facing down the toughest team in the conference for a berth on the ship heading to state-tournament glory.

All of our pictures were in the paper, and each of us got a column describing his life history. The nervous juices started eating away at my stomach on

Monday, making my chances of actually living until Friday seem somewhat remote.

When the day finally came, it was a blur. In Spanish I noticed that the afternoon sky had darkened, and by the time school let out, a spattery, cold rain was falling from the dun-colored sky.

The Big Guy up there wasn't making it easy for us.

Mrs. Knutson looked like a gnome in her pink raincoat with the pointy hood.

"I'm going to stay nice and dry—and warm," she said, modeling for us.

"But Chan," said Young. "Are they still going to have a game? It looks pretty bad out there." Indeed, outside, rain was beating on the windows as if it wanted to be let in.

"There are no rain dates in football," I told her.

"No indeedy, it's not for the faint of heart—players or fans," Mrs. Knutson said as she showed us her newest "Go Miners!" acquisition. "Normally these fanny warmers are for hunting and ice fishing. You just break these two packs of chemicals, and when they mix, there's this chemical reaction that will warm up the pad. Course, you can't see the 'Go Miners!' thing when you're sitting on it, but that's the breaks."

"Is it safe?" Young asked.

"Oh my, yes. It doesn't get *that* hot." Mrs. K. giggled. "So you go out and get 'em tonight, Chan!"

"I will," I promised, checking to make sure I had my soccer shoes, although neither football or soccer shoes worked particularly great on a wet field.

ALL-PRO's horn bleated outside. Young jumped as much as I did.

"Good luck, Oppa," she said as I ran out the door into the rain.

It was good that Moose Creek was one of the closer schools—one and a half hours—because you can get awful tired sitting on a bus.

Today's ride was eerie. No one spoke; we just watched the ghastly green light from the bus's dashboard, listened to the *squee-squee* of wipers in a losing battle against an army of drops.

The bullet-holed glass still hadn't been changed in the school's door. It was déjà vu all over again as Leland crept into the shower and Mikko sat around with his Walkman on.

Before we went out, Coach called for a prayer.

"I don't do that stuff," said Jimmi. "I'm Indian. I don't pray to no white man's god." He looked at me. "How 'bout you—don't you pray to Buddha or something?"

I thought of the long, elaborate graces Abogee said. *Heavenly Father, we thank you for our home, for the children, for Korea, for this food, for Chia pets, etc. . . . etc.*

"Jimmi," I said, "I have this feeling they're all the

same guy—or whatever—somewhere down the line. Prayer's fine with me."

Coach gave me a grateful nod and said a quick prayer, not to Jesus, or Muhammad, or the Great Spirit, or anyone in particular, just to that force that was watching over us. He hoped he/she/it would give us strength.

Leland Farrell kept his eyes closed the longest, after Coach finished up.

Outside, the rain drummed steadily on our bare heads as we stood, helmets tucked beneath our arms, for the National Anthem. I was cheered to see the stands on our side almost as full as the Moose Creek side.

We lost the toss. It was going to be an uphill battle all the way.

The coaches positioned the defense for Moose Creek's classic drives up the middle. But after the first play, they saw that the Spartans were copying our wishbone offense. Coach quickly grouped more guys to the outside.

We held them at their thirty, and they punted.

The kick was short because of the wind, and Jimmi squatted like he was catching a pumpkin. Before anyone knew what was happening, he had gone twenty yards through the slop.

"We're set up perfectly, thanks to Beargrease's nice

return," Coach said. It was third down, on Moose Creek's five-yard line. "Chan, you're going in at half-back. We're going to run that short play-action pass we ran Thursday." ALL-PRO was put in as quarterback with me.

ALL-PRO called the signals. I was the primary receiver; the wide receiver was going out as a decoy. I prayed he would get double coverage.

"Hike!"

A big old hole opened up. Thank God for Rom. I ran through, then evaded another Spartan by faking right while twisting. A classic soccer move. The guy got a handful of air.

I careened into the end zone, turned.

The football, a most gorgeous object, was heading right for me.

Please, God. Don't let me drop it. . . .

Right between the numbers. It was wet, and I bent my entire body over it and squeezed as hard as I could.

"Yaaahhh!" I didn't realize I was yelling.

"Yah!" from our side. Toots of sonic horns.

Then I lined up for the extra point.

"Gonna get you," snarled one of the Spartans as he panted. "Chink."

When the ball was snapped, Moose Creek converged on me like a pack of wolves. It was hard for me to plant my foot in the mud and slippery grass, and the kick went wide, dinging off the left upright, something that had never happened to me before.

"Hoser!" someone from the other side called.

"Don't worry, Chan," Coach said. "We'll make it up later."

But when was later? The Spartans drove us back for a touchdown, 6–7, ahead now because *they* made the extra point. We rallied to make it 13–7, but it was 13–14 going into the half.

"It's up to you, gentlemen," said Coach quietly. We were all sullenly staring at the lime-green walls, trying to get up the courage to go out there and play the second half.

Kearny stepped forward. He didn't look so happy.

"I don't want to hear any complaints about the weather, either," he stormed. "It's raining and blowing on them just as much."

He suddenly whirled and grabbed Leland's face mask, pulled him eye to eye.

"So what's with the dropped snaps, Farrell? This is not the time to be making such stupid mistakes."

"Yes, sir," Leland said miserably.

Coach stepped in.

"I know you're all wet, tired, and cold, but do you want to go home as wet and tired conference champs, or losers?"

It was obvious, to us.

The rain had not let up at all. In fact, if you looked up at the stadium lights, it appeared to be coming down in sheets. I didn't understand how the air could be so cold and still not produce snow.

The band people and the fans were miserably huddled under ponchos. I made out the pink, pointy head of Mrs. Knutson, Mr. Ripanen's blaze-orange parka.

We *couldn't* lose. There were too many people counting on us.

In the third quarter we spun our wheels on offense. On a third down Leland came back to the sidelines with his right hand cupped inside his left.

"Some weeg stomped on it in the pile," he growled. "Where the hell are the refs?"

"Son, that finger's dislocated," said Doc Larson. When he held it up to the light, Leland's pinky dangled like a Vienna sausage.

Coach stalked down the sideline, haranguing the zebras. When he came back, the game resumed. No call for unnecessary roughness.

The rain drummed on my helmet. We were going to need an ark to get home if this kept up.

Time to punt. My fingers were so cold, they felt like carrots as I caught the snap, barely managing to hold on to the ball. My left foot searched desperately for traction on the slick ground as I got it away.

A few plays later, their quarterback managed to get a drippy pass into the end zone.

"No!" I found myself screaming.

The buzzer sounded the end of the quarter, 13–22. They had completed a two-point conversion. Like last time.

"We're not dead yet," Coach told us. Everyone's eyes kept gravitating over to ALL-PRO, now that Leland was out.

"You . . . " Coach said to Rom. "You protect Ripanen. And Kim, too, when he's kicking. This next quarter is going to depend on them."

Rom nodded slowly, didn't look at me or Mikko.

ALL-PRO carried and passed.

He got us a first down, then another. Jimmi was a wonder at running through the mud. He got us to Moose Creek's three yard line. So tantalizingly close, my feet were curled up in my cleats with frustration as much as cold.

"Set!"

All of us on the bench craned our necks to see.

We all heard a bloodcurdling scream as Rom toppled the players in front of him like so many dominoes. ALL-PRO went flying—*doot-doot-doot!*—like the Six-Million-Dollar Man, over Rom's back into the end zone. He rolled on a shoulder and got up, still cradling the ball.

Our side went crazy. "Mi-ners! Mi-ners!"

175

"Go, Chan."

I squeegeed my way onto the field.

"Chink!" I heard, this time from the stands. "Chingchong!" The whole town of Moose Creek seemed to be drooling for my blood.

Mikko put the snap down exactly where he was supposed to.

I slipped, but not enough to keep the pigskin from hobbling through the uprights. The ref raised his arms.

"Almost gotcha," said one of the Spartan rushers closest to me. "Next time, chingchong boy, you're gonna hurt."

I kept my eyes on the scoreboard.

20–22.

Damn!

The clock was ticking.

"Channer," said ALL-PRO, "if we can get the ball to the thirty, can you make the field goal?"

The dreaded field goal. Just thinking about it made my ribs hurt. On a dry field I couldn't always do it. Now the field was an oil slick.

ALL-PRO's eyes were almost luminous beneath his helmet.

"Get the ball there. I'll kick it in."

thirty

You know that scene in *The Wizard of Oz* where Dorothy has to watch the hourglass of her life run out? That's how I felt, keeping one eye on the field, one eye on the clock, and shivering so hard that I bit my lip to bleeding. We had possession, we were creeping down the field, but oh so slowly.

How was I going to kick in this slippery goo, even if we did get down there? Neither the soccer or football cleats provided any traction.

Barefoot.

Like in tae kwon do. A natural kick.

I've kicked through boards before, with my instep. It might hurt a little, but that goes away.

Tentatively I took off my left shoe and sock and planted my foot in the freezing muck. I gripped the earth with my toes.

Less than two minutes to the final gun. But ALL-PRO was almost there. He ran the ball in himself to the twenty-eight.

"You ready, Chan?"

I nodded.

Kearny looked at me and my bare feet like I'd lost my mind, but Coach merely patted me on the helmet. I did a few roundhouse kicks in the air to loosen my hips.

"Chan! Chan! Chan!" our side yelled.

"We're there, buddy," ALL-PRO said as I joined the line. "We'll cover you. Don't worry 'bout a thing."

"Remember to turn the laces," I said, although I knew he would.

"Where ya shoes—jap?" came a call from the Spartan side. "He thinks he's Bruce Lee."

I was so used to all that crap from Rom and Jimmi, it didn't even make me annoyed. My eyes never left the place where ALL-PRO was going to set the snap. I lined up the hash marks, marked my place, felt the wind on my cheeks. If I could get this kick off, the wind would help it along. I just had to get it off.

The Spartans started howling like a kennel of dogs. But above that, I heard a slightly soggy C-note. A vote of confidence from Young.

I gave the signal that I was ready.

The rest was a blur.

When I kicked, my left foot dug hard into the ground, like I was a one-legged bird trying to stay on a branch. My right leg went up high on the follow-through. The connection felt right. There were big yellow uniforms hurtling toward me, but I knew it was too late for them to stop the ball.

Everyone carried me on their shoulders—even Rom and Jimmi. Once we started screaming, we couldn't stop. Someone dumped a whole barrel of muddy water on Kearny, and he just laughed.

I went over to the stands to see Rainey. Her hair was plastered to her face in dark ringlets.

"I'll see you at the parking lot at school when we get back, okay?"

She just smiled.

We got in late, still making noise. Coach said we needed to go straight home and rest. He was serious.

"What? We're not going out and celebrating?" I whispered to ALL-PRO. "How can that be?"

"We're going to *State*, Chan. You won't believe how good those teams from the Cities are. We really do have to rest up."

"But for a month?"

"You'll see," he said.

Rainey was waiting out in the parking lot.

"I'm sorry," I told her. "The boss says we can't go out."

"For real?"

"For real. The coaches will cruise around town,"

ALL-PRO said, and he opened the passenger side of the Probe. "See ya, Rainey."

We managed to get in one quick kiss, tasting of rain.

"I'll call you tomorrow."

We arrived chez Kim just as Donna was pulling in with her funny yellow car that looked like a newer version of Leland's Hunchback.

"Hey, Young," said Mikko.

Young looked scared, confused. The lights in the house were off. Lou wasn't in the driveway.

"Young, they're not here," I said. *"Lou's not in the driveway."*

ALL-PRO looked surprised to hear me blabbering away in Korean.

"They're going to come back soon, I bet."

"Who knows? Sometimes they work late."

"I said I wasn't going to see him. We already talked about it."

"This isn't a date. It's a coincidence. O-Ma and Abogee can't fault you for that. I'll watch for you, anyway."

"Donna," I said, walking up to her and bowing like an Englishman. "Would you like a spot of tea before your long, cold journey home?"

"I'd be most delighted," she said.

We left Young and Mikko outside. Inside I boiled water and dug out a tea bag. Mrs. Knutson had left us some peanut-butter cookies, so I put a few of those on a plate.

We carried the tea to the living room and turned on the TV down low so as not to wake Mrs. Knutson, and we watched some late movie.

The street was quiet, as usual. That was good. When Lou, the clanker and wanker, came within two miles of the house, we'd hear him.

About half an hour later I peered out the curtains. Young and Mikko were huddled together so closely, they looked like one glob. I think they might have been kissing, but I closed the curtain before I could determine that. I didn't really want to know what they were doing, to tell you the truth.

A minute later Young came into the house.

"Mikko said he'll call you tomorrow," she said, her voice sounding uplifted.

"I guess I'd better go." Donna got up. "Congratulations, Chan. I don't usually pay attention to the games we play at, but I was glad I did today. Awesome kick—was that a field goal?"

I nodded. "Thanks. See ya."

I didn't feel like going to sleep. Not after such a glorious game.

"Let's play cards," I said to Young.

"Thanks, Oppa," she said.

"For asking you to play cards?"

"No, silly. You know. For helping me out."

"I'm your oppa. It's my job to look out for you," I said. "Besides, then you'll owe me. So how about a game of War?"

"No way, Oppa, that is such a stupid game," she said, but then she took a look at my puppy-dog face and relented. I happily split the deck in half.

"You know," Young said as she slapped her cards on top of mine, "maybe it wasn't such a horrible thing coming here. I really like Donna and some of the kids here. And back in L.A. we always had so much pressure to do better than the other kids, don't you think?"

Young was talking about the *Korean* kids. Back in L.A., everyone's parents whipped everyone into a frenzy about whose kids were doing the best. We always had to endure constant news reports of who got great SAT scores, who got accepted early decision to Harvard, who found the cure for cancer. It was like, hint, hint, why aren't *you* doing that great, huh? I'm surprised we didn't all end up killing each other.

"I think O-Ma and Abogee are less uptight here too," she said.

"Well," I said. "At college-application time next year, it might be a different story." For our birthday O-Ma and Abogee had given us SAT prep books. Young had the *Princeton Review* and I had *Barron's*. We were supposed to swap them when we finished. Not everything had changed.

"I just feel so much freer here," Young said, the dim light from a lamp glinting off her eyes. "Like maybe it's good to get away from all the Koreans. Here we're different and special."

"I have news for you, Sis," I said. "You'd be special even without all those prizes. Just ask Mrs. Knutson—she adores you."

Young blushed. "Thanks, Oppa. You're pretty special too."

It was a pretty goopy moment. Fortunately, a war with cards kept things from getting too sloppy.

When O-Ma and Abogee came home at about one o'clock, we were still up playing. They were like, oh, you're still up, but they seemed glad to see us, like the vision of Young and me playing cards in the living room of a borrowed home was just about the best thing in the world.

thirty-one

Mikko and I were on the football field all by our lonesomes. The coaches had generously given us a whole day off to rest before the *real* killer workouts were to begin.

Mikko still wanted to practice. It had been raining cats and dogs earlier but had stopped, so I went along with him. Besides, the girls' tennis team was playing their last game away, so it wasn't like I'd be missing time with Rainey.

I noticed Mikko kept looking out to the street side of the field, all during practice.

"Young said she might stop by," he finally admitted. He looked so glum, I felt bad for him.

"Don't sweat it, man," I said. "She probably got held up at band or something. They have to practice more now too."

Frankly, I didn't want to get involved. I mean, when they get married, I'll be the first to toast them. But keep me out of the messy details, *please*.

"Look," I added. "Young never goes for ugly football players, so she must really like you. Not to mention that she's not supposed to date until college."

"That's nuts."

"Tell me about it. Rainey's parents have me over for dinner all the time, but then I have to be like, well, uh, no, in fact, you can't come over."

ALL-PRO cracked half a smile. "See, you're sneaky."

"What's right is relative," I said. I tossed him the ball, an easy spiral, but for some reason he dropped it.

Somewhere in town a siren sounded.

Then another, more drawn-out. *RRRrrr, RRRRrrrr.*

"Fire truck," ALL-PRO said.

"Hope it's not Mom and Mrs. Knutson," I said. The other day the two of them had been up to some culinary experiment that failed, and it made so much smoke, I thought the fire trucks were going to come. Luckily Mrs. Knutson thought to dump a box of baking soda on top of it.

"I'm feeling a little bushed. Let's go home," Mikko said suddenly.

There was a smell of pot roast—unburned—in the house when I got home.

"Where's Young?" Her shoes weren't by the door.

"She's out with Donna," O-Ma said. "She should be home by five thirty."

I went upstairs to put my stuff away.

At five forty-five O-Ma joked about withholding dinner from Young.

But she didn't return by six, or six thirty. She was never late. Always "on the dot," as Mrs. Knutson would say. She always called.

By seven we knew something was wrong. O-Ma called Abogee, and he came home from the store. We were all sitting silently in the living room. No one moved except for Mrs. Knutson, who was attempting to do some knitting but was strangling whatever it was she was making.

The phone rang. We all fell over each other trying to get it. I won.

It was Mrs. Leschke, Donna's mother, wondering if Donna was over here.

"No, she's not. Young isn't back either." I barely whispered into the phone. As I hung up I said a silent prayer. *Please, God, let Young be all right. I know she's never late, but let her and Donna be out playing some stupid prank for once. That's all I ask.*

The doorbell rang. A man in a police uniform was there. He said he was Joe Skotvold, chief of the Iron River Police.

I let him in, stiffly, formally, as though he were a guest and we were expecting him.

"My daughter," O-Ma said, half rising. "My daughter Young. Do you know—"

Sometimes these things just come and you can't stop them.

In between the words *Your daughter Young* and the rest of the sentence, *was killed,* hung the most ghastly silence I have ever experienced in my life.

Someone was yelling, screaming. There was the sound of things breaking. Make them stop, I was thinking. I put my hands over my ears. Make it stop.

It took two slaps from Abogee to bring me back.

When I opened my eyes, it was like observing a scene in a wax museum. O-Ma and Mrs. Knutson were huddled motionlessly together on the couch. The policeman stood with his eyes to the floor. Abogee paused, hand still raised.

Young was dead.

She was *not* dead.

She *couldn't* be dead.

I am going to contest this play, I was thinking. Show me the instant replay. I am going to contest this play.

I kept repeating that, over and over and over. It was the only way I had of keeping my head from blowing apart into a million pieces.

thirty-two

We had to go to the hospital to identify the body. Young and Donna had been in a car accident. The doctor said she was going to be hard to look at. He suggested only Abogee go in.

"She's my daughter too," O-Ma said. I took her hand. We all went in, as a family.

We met Donna's parents outside her hospital room. Donna had broken her back, but she was in stable condition. Thank God for small favors and seat belts, I was thinking with one side of my brain. The other side was practically screaming with jealousy. Why did Donna get to live, and not Young? Why?

Abogee and O-Ma were on the phone constantly, to L.A. and Korea. When they hung up, the phone rang again. Once, Mikko called; once, Rainey did. I told them I couldn't talk right now, and I acted like I had something pressing to do. Of course it was a lie. Nothing was pressing anymore.

The doorbell rang. I made the mistake of answering it, thinking it might be flowers or someone bringing food.

But no. It was ALL-PRO.

"I don't want to talk right now," I said, starting to close the door.

He put his hand in the jamb.

"But I do."

I hadn't talked to ALL-PRO since before the accident, I realized. The last time he was actually *inside* the house was when the three of us watched TV that time. I couldn't believe it. I let him in.

"Have you seen Donna?" he asked.

I nodded.

"Did she tell you what happened?" He looked different, like his cheekbones poked out more or something.

"She said she swerved to miss a deer and the car hit a slick patch. The deer lived."

"What were they doing on the highway?"

"Cruising, I guess. She just got her license."

"Was she a good driver?"

"How should I know?" I said. "Why are you asking me all this?"

"I just want to know. I don't know a thing about what happened except what I saw in the paper. So was Donna a good driver?"

"Hell if I know," I said. "It's not like things will change if you figure out exactly what happened. My sister's gone, Mikko, gone."

"I just have to know," ALL-PRO said. His eyes were red. He slammed his fists into each other.

"Young's dead," I said. The tonelessness of my voice surprised even me. "The end."

ALL-PRO grabbed me by my shoulders.

"Goddammit, Chan! You're not the only person who's lost someone. What about your parents? What about *me*?"

"So I'll put you out of your misery too. My father owns a gun." I put a nice layer of sarcasm on top of everything, to hide my true intentions, whatever they were.

"Don't do anything stupid, Chan." ALL-PRO's eyes were practically boring through my head. His nostrils were white. I tried to put myself in his shoes, to experience *his* loss of Young, but I couldn't. Mine loomed too large. Way too large.

"I'm sorry" was all I could say to him.

Suddenly Mikko leaned over and touched my hair, like you do with a little kid who needs soothing.

"We gotta be there for each other, buddy," he said. "That's all any of us can do."

thirty-three

The house was beginning to fill with people. The Kims, the Lees, the Parks—SuJin's parents. And SuJin. Those were the people who could afford to come out here. None of the people in Korea could.

Abogee had called his brother, Bong, now living in Milwaukee. He was supposed to be coming too.

All of them brought food. Korean food. I had basically stopped eating since the accident—we all had—but the longed-for smells of *kimchi* and *namul* vegetables were too much for me.

"My, you really like that, don't you?" Mrs. Knutson put one birdlike hand on my shoulder as she peered at the red peppery, garlicky, sesame-seedy expanse of veggies, meat, and rice before me.

"Glug," I said, mouth full.

Mrs. K. had been amazing in all of this, arranging the funeral at her church, cleaning the house, holding O-Ma's hand for hours on end. O-Ma had barely come out of her room since the accident.

Now Mrs. K. was going to stay with a friend so we could have more room, especially when Bong showed up. We would all be meeting at the funeral.

Bong arrived by bus right into Iron River, at the Gas 'n' Carry. Abogee and I went to pick him up.

He was the same old Bong, hair sticking up like a rooster's comb, watery smile. He didn't say anything other than "Hi" when we picked him up. Abogee didn't say anything either.

O-Ma asked me if I might say a few words at Young's funeral, but I refused. How could I possibly begin to tell anyone what it was like to lose a person who was more than just a sister—who was more like half of me? I didn't know what to tell myself.

I said I'd let SuJin speak for me. She was good at putting things into pretty words; she'd be able to tell people what a good person Young was.

The house rustled with people moving to and fro, but there was barely a murmur of voices. I put on my sports coat and khakis, my one good outfit. As I dug around for my good shoes, I came across my soccer shoes, still covered in mud from the last game. That game seemed an eternity ago, and so small somehow. I couldn't believe I had put so much time and energy into chasing after a stupid football.

When everyone was downstairs, I slipped into Young's room. I almost held my breath when I was in there, panicky that I'd detect some scent, some trace of warmth from when my sister was alive. But there was none.

Her room was impeccable: the bed made, the desk clear with her books stacked, pencils neatly gathered in a GO MINERS! mug. The Korean quilts were completely smooth.

I spied what I'd come for, grabbed it, and ran, shutting the door tightly behind me.

O-Ma began to cry before we even reached the church steps. Abogee and I had to help her into the sand-colored building, the First Lutheran Church of Iron River. Her arm felt as light and fragile as a bird's wing in my hand.

Donna's parents were there, but Donna was still in the hospital. Mr. Goeske, our math teacher, kneeled in a pew, apparently praying. Rainey waved sadly at me when she saw me. So did ALL-PRO. I waved back, got into the viewing line.

I didn't want to see my sister dead. The idea of an open casket is barbaric to me.

But there was something I knew I had to do.

When my turn came, I kept my eyes on the brass handles of the casket, and carefully laid Young's flute in it.

*   *   *

The wailing.

Mrs. Park and Mrs. Kim and Mrs. Lee just started wailing, *"Aiii-gu!" "Aiii-gu!" "Aiii-gu!"* and flailing their arms around.

Other people in church, including the Reverend Mr. Hanson, jumped, then stared, like they weren't sure what was going on.

"Aiii-gu!" "Aiii-gu!"

O-Ma had done this at Halmoni's funeral, but not this loud, this intense. The air-raid noise went on without stopping for even a second, and I started to feel like it was going to burst my head from the inside.

"Aii-gu!" "Aii-gu!"

Make them stop! I wanted to shout. But when I looked over at O-Ma and Abogee, half expecting them to have their hands over their ears, I saw that they looked strangely calmed, as if these women were doing the noisy and messy grieving they couldn't themselves.

Finally the Reverend Mr. Hanson ascended to the pulpit, and the women stopped.

The reverend said some words on death and dying, but I didn't listen. He didn't know Young at all. Everything he said reeked of fakeness—especially when he said things like "this young woman meant so much to all of us."

SuJin got up next. She was carrying a Korean-English Bible, just like Abogee's. She was pale, her black eyes liquid. She opened the Bible on its ribbon and began to read.

> *"For everything there is a season, and a time for*
> *every matter under heaven.*
> *A time to be born, and a time to die;*
> *a time to plant, and a time to pluck up what is*
> *planted;*
> *a time to kill, and a time to heal;*
> *a time to break down, and a time to build up;*
> *a time to weep, and a time to laugh;*
> *a time to mourn, and a time to dance;*
> *a time to cast away stones, and a time to gather*
> *stones together; . . .*
> *a time to seek, and a time to lose; . . .*
> *He has put eternity into men's mind, yet so that*
> *he cannot find out what God has done from*
> *the beginning to end. . . . That which is,*
> *already has been; and God seeks what has*
> *been driven away."*

Jesus. SuJin. Corny, even in her grief.

I wished it would rain, or snow, or do something as we filed out for the trip to the cemetery. But the sky was clear. It wouldn't be long, though, before the ground was completely frozen.

We all stood and stared at the casket. Everyone in our family was going to bow, in reverse order. The women started wailing, but more quietly this time, as I walked in front of the casket. Since I could remember, I had bowed to my parents every *Saehae*, New Year's, so I sank to my knees and performed a bow without even thinking about how to do it. If Young's spirit was truly around somewhere, she'd probably be laughing at me, practically shoving my face in the dirt for her.

O-Ma and Abogee went next, together. O-Ma, supported by Mrs. Park and Mrs. Lee, did a small dip; I could see tears silently flowing down her face. I was thinking of this Korean proverb that Halmoni had told me: *"When parents die, you bury them in the ground. When children die, you bury them in your heart."*

All of a sudden Abogee jumped up from the ground and threw himself on top of the casket. A few people gasped.

I was stuck to the spot. I was half hoping Abogee would howl and moan and shout and curse the gods so loud that the sky would split open.

But he was just crying, making tiny animal noises. I'd never seen his face look so shattered, so broken. The whole world seemed to stop. No one knew what to do.

Finally Mr. Park went up to Abogee and touched his shoulder. Mr. Park murmured something and then gently supported Abogee as he led him away from the casket.

The casket was lowered, and each of us was given a chance to put a shovelful of dirt on top of it.

I felt a hand on my shoulder and jumped. I looked, but no one was there. O-Ma and Abogee were both watching the casket, the tears now dry on their faces. There was no breeze.

Then it was over. Mikko came and gave me a bone-crunching hug. I held on to him like he was a tree. I was grateful he didn't say anything. I couldn't stand any more words.

thirty-four

"Who's that guy?" Mikko stared at Bong, who was shoveling hotdish into his mouth about as fast as it would go.

"My uncle Bong, the first owner of Froggie's."

ALL-PRO picked apart of piece of *potica*, this layered dessert bread that someone had brought.

"How come you guys came up here after he left?"

"Like I told you, Bong went crazy for some other get-rich-quick scheme and took off, leaving us holding the bag with the franchise."

"So you didn't know, then."

"Know what?"

"That the cops were planning to raid the place. For drugs."

"Holy—You've got to be kidding." So that explained the nervous, edgy guys who kept coming into the store asking for Bong, or asking for some unknown product that we were supposed to have and know by its code name, huh-huh-huh or whatever.

"I guess when he skipped town, he ticked off the druggies who had outstanding orders. So they trashed the store."

"Ah," I said. "The cinderblocks."

"What?"

"Oh, there were a bunch of cinderblocks in the middle of the store. I'd always wondered how they got there."

"I can't say for sure if there really was something going on," ALL-PRO said, "but you know how word travels in town. So when you guys showed up, a lot of people thought we were in for more of the same—someone from the outside bringing drugs and stuff in."

"Oh, great," I said. "Is that what you thought?"

"No, not after I got to know you," he said. "Honest. Like I said, when you play on a team with someone, you end up knowing what their real character is like."

"And?"

"I wouldn't be your friend if you were a craphead drug dealer."

Bong left later that day. What he had to rush back to, I didn't know. On the car ride to the bus station I casually mentioned to him that people had come into the store looking for him. He ignored me.

"People keep asking for this stuff, if we carry it, huh-huh-huh, *or something like that."*

"I am very tired," Bong said. *"It has been a long day."*

"What about the rent?" I pushed. *"We came here and found out you owed two months' rent on your apartment."*

Bong smoothed his greasy hair, lit up a cigarette, and blew smoke out the window.

"Stop bothering your uncle," Abogee said.

"Did Uncle ever explain why the store was in such bad shape?" I asked Abogee on the drive back.

His jaw tightened.

"I think he had some enemies in town."

"The less you speak, the better," he said.

O-Ma and Abogee drove the L.A. guests to the airport in the next town, and then we were all by ourselves again.

Our house looked like a greenhouse. Even though we'd put a little notice in the obituary not to send stuff, people we didn't even know brought enamel dishes wrapped up in white cloths that said SWEDISH LADIES' HOTDISH CLUB. Some people sent cards to Mrs. Knutson with cash in them.

"People here want to help," she told me. She passed the cards on to O-Ma and Abogee and secretly put the money in a savings account and gave me the passbook. "You will need this for college," she said.

thirty-five

Five thirty. Time to go to practice. Two-a-days and weight training. *We have a long journey ahead of us,* Coach said in my dream. *Might as well enjoy the ride.*

I blinked. Football didn't mean the same thing to me anymore. What was different? I was tired. So tired.

Seven o'clock. Time to get up for school.

Seven thirty. Need to leave for school.

Seven fifty. It's too late. Why can't I get up?

Because I'm waiting for Young. I'm waiting for her to come up here and say, "Yo! Get your lazy butt out of bed, Oppa. I know you're not sick, just avoiding reality."

But she's not here. She's gone. Forever.

I pulled the covers over my head, closed my eyes, and slept for another few hours.

When I just couldn't sleep anymore, I wandered around the house. O-Ma and Abogee were gone. They'd left me a note saying I didn't have to go to school. Mrs. Knutson was out somewhere too. She'd left me a pile of peanut-butter-and-honey sandwiches, some wild-rice-and-sausage hotdish. The house was quiet. So quiet.

I grabbed the sandwiches off the counter.

I walked into school just as classes were breaking for lunch. All eyes were on me, like I was a rare butterfly impaled under glass. This time I wasn't Chan the New Boy Who Is Also Asian. I was Chan the Kid Who Lost His Sister.

The crowd parted like the Red Sea to let me pass. I wanted to tell them death wasn't catching. My feet, through force of habit, made their way to the gym.

The guys looked at me like I was Jesus, or Lazarus, or Elvis after the resurrection. Take your pick.

"Hi," said ALL-PRO.

"Hey, Chan," said Leland. Everyone else was silent. Staring.

"So I guess you're not coming to practice, huh?" ALL-PRO said to me after lunch.

I shook my head. "Are you?"

"I don't know. Haven't gone all week."

My perception of things had totally changed, the way a kaleidoscope does when you twist the knob. Football had once been the center of my universe. Now, with life and death intruding, I saw it for what it was: a colossal waste of time. It shouldn't have ever mattered, but it had. So I was stupid and Abogee had been right all along.

"You're not actually thinking about going, are you?"

ALL-PRO studied his Sambas. "I think it might help, you know. The team needs us. No use sitting around feeling sorry for ourselves."

Everything was coming to a slow, rolling stop.

"Young is dead and you're thinking about play-ing *football*?" Gray spots began to dance before my eyes.

"Chan, listen. I know she's dead. We can't do any-thing about it." ALL-PRO's hand, holding a carton of milk, trembled, and a few white drops spilled out. "So why can't we finish what we started on the field? This means a lot to us, to the town."

"I can't believe this! She's not even cold in the ground and it's just business as usual for you. I thought you loved her."

A vein throbbed in Mikko's temple. His skin was so pale, I could see it clearly.

"I did love her. More than you realize." ALL-PRO's voice, usually so low, was strained comically high. "So playing ball has always helped me deal with things. It might even keep me from hurting myself. Is that all right, Your Highness?"

"Yeah, sure. Do whatever the hell you want, you shallow jerk." I wheeled around and sprinted away, knocking people over like tenpins. Maybe it was a mistake to come back to school, but I didn't know, for the life of me, where to go.

So I went to Spanish.

I was surprised to see Coach waiting outside the door when the last class ended. He was leaning easily against the lockers, Mr. Casual himself. I blinked.

"How are you, son?"

I shrugged.

"Mind if I walk with you?"

"Sure, whatever." There was no way *he* was going to try to get me to come back to football.

"I'm sorry about your sister. I didn't know her too well—knew she was an outstanding math student—but I am very sorry."

"I am too," I said. My stock answer. I mean, with everyone coming up to you and saying they're sorry—when you're beyond sorry—what are you supposed to say?

"Do you have some time to talk?" he said, stopping, as the escaping kids streamed all around us.

"Sure," I said.

"How does Helga's Café sound?"

"Don't you have to go to practice?"

"Kearny's there. It's not a problem."

At Helga's I had a hot chocolate. Coach drank cups and cups of coffee. I could tell they hadn't put enough grounds in it. It probably tasted weak and sour. You get good at gauging these things when you work at a convenience store.

"So what do you want to talk about?"

"Nothing in particular," Coach said, lifting the chipped cup to his lips yet again. On the far wall an enormous fish was hanging, mouth open, like it was about to chomp on a fly. "I'd like to know how you're doing, how your family's doing."

"About as well as you'd expect." I placed the hot chocolate in front of me like a barrier.

"What was your sister like?"

"She wasn't someone you could describe in ten minutes." The words were so rude, I wished immediately I could take them back. I sighed. "I'm sorry. She was the best, that's all. It's hard to talk about."

Coach looked me in the eye.

"Chan, I just want you to know that I'm here for you. And the team is too."

I couldn't look at him. So I looked at his hands, instead. They were tapping the coffee cup. The nails were square, clipped, perfectly clean.

What was I doing here? Too much more of this and I was going to bawl like a baby. I didn't want him to know how close I was to breaking. To distract myself, I started to blab. I blabbed about Young, about being a twin. About how hard it was to leave L.A. Once the words spilled out, they kept coming, like they had a life of their own. Before I knew it, I'd blabbed about what had happened in the locker room that cold, lonely day.

When I looked up, Coach's face scared me.

"Who do you think jumped you?" he breathed.

I sat up. I'd somehow expected Coach not to listen too closely.

"I honestly don't know." It was true. I didn't, really. Okay, maybe there was also some warped sense of loyalty in that answer, but what proof did I have?

"Chan, you have to help me out. I don't know what-all goes on in the locker room."

"I didn't see anything," I said. "What would you be able to do with some wild guess?"

"Get to the bottom of this. I don't want any boy— *any* boy—who engages in that kind of conduct to have the privilege of playing on the team. I mean it. I have to know."

I focused on my own fingers, nails bitten to the quick. I found myself wishing I'd left something to bite.

"Don't let me down on this one, son," Coach said. His eyes were boring two holes into my skull. I would have liked to get up and run screaming from the table, but I was trapped. I tried to distract myself by concentrating on my breathing. No good. It was as if a huge vacuum cleaner had come in and sucked all the air out of Helga's Café.

"Okay, then," Coach said, spreading out his two

hands. "I'm just going to start naming names. It wasn't Sanderson, was it?"

I had an insane urge to laugh. Yeah, right.

"Leland Farrell?"

Coach ticked the names off his fingers. Like bullets. *Pow-pow-pow!*

"I guess Beargrease is about all that's left," he said. "Is he the one?"

I didn't nod, or shake my head, or move in any way. It didn't matter. It was like he could read my mind.

He sighed. "Okay."

But then he looked down and saw he had one finger left. He'd missed one last guy.

"Kreeger?" He sounded like he was going to choke.

Don't move, I told myself. Don't let on.

A little necessary roughness, huh?

I shook my head.

But I think Coach knew. Somehow he must have just known.

There was no denying the disappointment on Coach's face. His mouth opened, like that mounted fish, as if he were groping for some explanation, some way to set things right. Everyone knew we couldn't win State without Rom.

He reached over and put a hand on my shoulder. From somewhere, dripping coffee fell on a burner and hissed.

"I'm going to take action on this immediately," he said, his voice grim. "And in the meantime, if there's anything you need, let me know."

His hand squeezed my shoulder.

What would life be like if Coach were my abogee? We could talk, really talk, and do stuff together, and I wouldn't always feel like I'd failed some mysterious test only Abogee knew the answers to. Lousy of me to think like that, huh?

"And Chan, if—by any chance—you want to come to practice, the team's waiting for you. But it's your decision and of course we'll respect it, whatever it is."

"Thanks," I said. "I know Mikko was thinking of going back. He kind of ticked me off."

Coach shook his head. "Haven't seen him. But maybe he'll be back, if he's anything like his father. Old Rip, whenever he was mad, or sad, or whatever, he would just come and let it all out on the field. Some guys are like that."

"I guess," I said. "All the fun's sort of gone out of it for me."

"I understand, son. I do. I just want you to know that you've still got your place on the team if you decide you want it."

By the time I got home it was getting dark. I put on my sneakers and sweats and went outside. I had no idea where I was going, I just ran, let the feel of my body jolting over the tar take over everything.

I was just hitting my stride when I noticed a car was slowing.

Beep! "Hey, Chan." It was Rainey. "Want a lift?"

Until that moment I hadn't realized how much I'd wanted to see her. I hopped in the car.

"I've been missing you," she said tentatively, as if she wasn't sure I'd remember who she was.

"I missed you, too."

"I wish there was something I could do."

"Don't do anything. And please, don't say you're sorry."

I slithered over and put a sweaty hand on her knee as she drove. She smelled like flowers—jasmine, maybe.

It was too cold to sit in the car, so I invited her in and we went up to my room.

In the semi-darkness we just sat, sharing body heat. I loved that I didn't have to talk to Rainey. If I stopped talking to SuJin for two minutes, she'd be all over me, asking What's wrong, what did I do? Not Rainey. She just grooved in the silences.

When we came down, I was a little surprised to see Abogee sitting in the living room. There was no car in the driveway, so he must have walked home.

When he saw us, he rose.

"You should never bring a girl up to your room," he said. *"You know better than that."*

Sometimes, just the sight of someone, like the way they happen to look at that particular minute, can set you off. I looked at Abogee and this awful feeling rose up in me, a feeling mixed up from the time he almost hit me, the way he told us we were moving, how he'd made Young feel so bad about wanting to date. Abogee just pulled this reaction out of me, the way pepper pulls a reaction out of your nose.

"Please speak English, Father," I said. "We have a guest."

Abogee was a pot right before the boil. He shook. It scared me, thrilled me.

"You heard what I said."

"Abogee, I don't care what you say anymore." Something inside me twisted violently. My nerves hummed like live wires.

"Chan—" Rainey reached for me, but then seemed to think better of it and backed off.

"Why do I have to be left with the disobedient child?" Abogee said.

"What are you saying?" I yelled. "That it would have been better if *I* had died instead of Young? If *you* hadn't made us move here, she'd still be alive—alive! It's all your fault—you and your stupid drug-dealer brother."

I turned to Rainey. "I think you'd better go." She nodded.

This was it, I decided. The walls were going to come down, the dams break. Abogee and I would finally have it out.

But it was like I'd taken a pin and deflated Abogee's spirit. *Pfft!* The fight drained from Abogee completely, and he turned and shuffled upstairs, leaving me alone.

I went back up to my room. There was still a faint trace of Rainey's perfume in the air, and it comforted me. I shut the door tight.

Later that night O-Ma called up, offering to bring me some dinner. I wasn't hungry.

I lay in bed, in the pitch-blackness. I saw the car, the yellow subcompact. I saw the two girls in it, giggling and talking. Then the deer stepping out in front of them, the car skidding on the road. I saw the fear on Young's face the split second before impact, that last second she was alive and feeling. And all she was feeling was pure terror.

Did she scream for someone? I couldn't help wondering. Did she call for me?

For the first time, I just lay there and cried.

thirty-six

I am on the field. In fact, I have the ball and a game's going on. I hear cheers and hoots, but I don't know which end zone I'm supposed to go for. Rom and Jimmi are laughing their heads off.

Everything is in slow motion. I want to yell to the coaches, ask which way to the end zone, but my mouth won't work. Cheers and wails are coming from all directions, and I realize that this is the important game. The One.

"Chan!" Young is there. She is in a yellow-and-white cheerleader's uniform. But our colors are red and black. And why in the world is she a cheerleader?

She is waving her pompoms like crazy, yelling, "Go, Chan! Go, Chan!" Suddenly I can see where the end zone is, and I take off toward it. She keeps on smiling and cheering, so I know I'm going the right way.

Cheers. Cheers. Cheers.

My alarm clock is ringing its head off.

I pack my soccer cleats in my bag as I head downstairs.

"Are you here, like for real?" ALL-PRO asked.

"No, I'm a ghost," I said, unpacking my stuff.

Rom and Jimmi weren't there to greet me. When I asked Mikko where they were, he said he didn't know. He'd seen them head off with Coach and that had been that.

"Hey, Kim! Get your butt in gear," Kearny yelled. Then he tipped the bill of his cap toward me. "We're glad you're back."

The locker room stank of rust, jock-itch medicine, and sweat. I couldn't believe how good it smelled.

Out on the field, the tennis courts were empty, and I started thinking about Rainey again. I was wondering if there was any chance that my life would get back to normal.

"Glad to see your appetite is back, young man," Mrs. Knutson said as she watched me shovel in pounds of tuna-fish-and-egg-noodle hotdish as if I were stoking a furnace.

I woke up in the middle of the night desperately needing to go to the bathroom. Because the bathroom is all the way downstairs, I usually try to go back to sleep. This time I figured I might as well get it over with.

There was a funny smell coming from the living room.

I saw a smiling face illuminated in the glow of small flames. It took me a second to see that Abogee was holding sticks of incense in front of the Buddha statue.

Was Abogee actually *praying* to the Buddha? In church school we had always been taught that to worship anything other than Jesus was betraying God.

"Abogee," I said quietly. He turned, slowly. The look on his face was remarkably calm.

"Are you—are you—um, what are you doing?"

The smoke from the incense slowly spiraled upward in curls.

"I am wishing your sister safe passage on her journey."

Young's photo, black ribbons running diagonally over its frame, smiled back at us.

"You think I'm an old, superstitious man, don't you?"

I shook my head. I didn't know what I thought.

"In Korea, this is what we always did to honor the dead, to wish their spirit safe passage to the next place. It's not meant to be an affront to Jesus Christ. No, in fact, in this way all religions are supposed to coexist peacefully, even help each other."

Abogee chuckled.

214

"You know the president of Korea? One of the first things he did when he moved into the Blue House was to take the Buddha statue out of the garden. After all, he is a good Christian man. But that year, all sorts of bad things happened in Korea—bridges collapsed, buildings fell—so much that the people start calling him the 'accident president.' So what does this man do? He has the Buddha statue put back, at night, of course, so people don't see. He is still a good Christian. He put the statue back just in case."

The lights from the candle and the incense cast a warm glow on Abogee's face and smoothed out some of his wrinkles.

"Now, with your sister, I believe her spirit has gone up to heaven, but this way I will make sure she has a pleasant journey, just in case. The Lees told me to send her some things she loved, so I burned some books for her. And then I thought about her flute. . . ."

The living room looked so different in shadow. All of a sudden I felt so far away from everything.

I reached out and put my hand on Abogee's shoulder. It was bony, slightly stooped.

"She has her flute, Abogee. I made sure of that."

thirty-seven

Jimmi was at practice the next day. Maybe Rom would show up too. Who knew? I just lowered my head and got down to business. I admit I did miss Rom's glass stomach. The end-of-practice sprints now seemed to take forever before someone puked.

Today I did the honors. It came out as watery gruel, not real, true puke. But we got to stop.

"Morning sickness," I joked as ALL-PRO and I started our extra laps.

"Hey, Chan, can I talk to you for a sec?" It was Jimmi.

I glanced at Mikko, who shrugged.

"Okay," I said.

We went over to the bleachers, strangely empty now that the home-game season was over. An old candy wrapper went blowing by like tumbleweed.

"Coach and I had a talk yesterday."

"Uh-huh." I couldn't look at him, so I stared at my shoes.

"About you getting jumped in the locker room."

"So you heard about it, huh?" I tried to not let my voice drip with sarcasm.

"I was in on it."

I took a breath. Something was swelling inside me. I concentrated on seeing how well I could lace my fingers together. It was just me and him, now, face-to-face. Oh, what I could do in a fair fight. His face could be mush in a minute.

"But I didn't go through with it."

"What? You liar."

"I didn't. It was Rom and some of his older druggie buddies you don't even know. He wanted to jump you, teach you a lesson."

"Teach me *what?*"

"Not to have such a swelled head."

Swelled head—me? Compared to *him?* Now, this was getting interesting.

"I admit I wasn't so crazy about you coming in to the team like that—I've been playing football since I was a freshman. It was like you come in, not knowing crap, and then boom! I'm on the bench."

"We're supposed to be a *team*," I said. "And don't forget, you guys asked *me.*"

"Ripanen asked you, not us."

"Whatever."

"Look, I just wanted to say I'm sorry about your sister, and about you being jumped. I could've done something about it, but I didn't. I told Coach all about it. I thought he was going to kick me off with Rom, but he didn't."

"I still don't believe you weren't in on it. What about the bruise I saw you with the next day?"

"What about it? Rom gave it to me. Right between the eyes when I said I wouldn't go."

If this was true, Jimmi was a sicker puppy than I'd thought.

"Explain one thing to me, then," I said. "Why the hell do you stay buddies with someone who punches you when you disagree with him?"

"Rom's not all bad," he said. "He just loses it too easy. He doesn't like new people. But you know, if not for him, I wouldn't even be able to play football."

I looked at him.

"We don't have a car, my dad and me. Rom, he gave me a ride every day. That's almost two hours for him. He helped me raise up the money to get a letter jacket, so I could be like the rest of you guys."

Jimmi spat. "You know, everyone at our school thinks Indians are scum. Teachers too. They don't care if we dry up and die on the res."

"So how are you getting home now?"

Jimmi started unpeeling some tape from his wrists.

"Coach, actually." He laughed a little when he saw the way I was looking at him. "Okay, so some teachers do care."

*   *   *

It would have been a perfect ending if we had shaken hands, or hugged, or gone to a sweat lodge or something together, but Jimmi just got up and left. I went back to Mikko.

"What was all that all about?" ALL-PRO said. "You look like Jimmi just gave you the secret recipe to Reddi Whip or something."

"He sort of did," I said. "A lot of unexpected ingredients."

thirty-eight

"I can get you some really good seats at the state tournament," I said tentatively.

Mrs. Knutson brightened. I knew she would love to get her hands on some tickets. O-Ma and Abogee didn't say a word.

"The state tournament is kind of a big deal."

"You better believe it," Mrs. Knutson said. "Ok-Hee, Sung-Ho, you might as well just close your store because no one's going to be in town. We haven't gone to a state tournament in ten years!"

"I'd like you all to come," I said. "It would kind of mean a lot to me if you could see me play."

A shadow passed over O-Ma's face.

"But Chan, it's hardly been three weeks since Young . . ."

"I know, O-Ma, I know," I said. "At first when Mikko was trying to get me to come back, I thought, That's crazy. But then I got to thinking. Just because Young died doesn't mean we should stop living. I mean, I don't think *she'd* want it that way." I hesitated. "Um, this might sound crazy, but the other night I dreamed about Young. I think she'd want me to play."

"Son," Abogee said. *"I think your mind has left you. Are you talking about ghosts? Spirits?"*

But his voice wasn't angry. It almost had a hint of a laugh in it.

"I believe in ghosts," Mrs. Knutson said firmly. "And angels, too." We all stared at her. How the heck had she understood what Abogee was saying?

"You will just love Minneapolis, I guarantee it," she went on. "It's such a beautiful city, so clean, so cultured."

"And we could stock up on some *kimchi*," I said.

"Yobo," Abogee said to O-Ma. "I think we should go. To watch our son—our only son."

"We will go," she said, finally.

"I'll buy three tickets," I said.

Abogee and O-Ma were going to see me play.

thirty-nine

The pep stuff continued to sell like gangbusters. Mrs. Knutson had gotten us some huge foam GO MINERS! pickaxes that the little kids loved to brain each other with. It seemed like no one came into the store without leaving with some.

Once, when I came to the store to work, I saw Abogee studying a book, *Understanding the Basics of Football*, which he shoved under the counter when he saw me. I pretended not to see, but inside I couldn't stop smiling.

O-Ma, Abogee, and Mrs. Knutson drove down to the Cities in her Chevy, since Lou's heater seemed to have permanently fritzed out. They stayed at the Tom Thumb Inn, where all the Iron River parents were, in adjoining rooms.

Minneapolis did have big buildings. It was amazing how I'd gotten used to the smallness of Iron River. I was right there with the other guys gawking at the

IDS Tower, which loomed over us, covered in swimming-pool-blue mirrors.

"Don't sunburn the roofs of your mouths," Kearny told us.

I couldn't help it. A mall where we stopped for some vitamins had three floors and seemed to go on forever.

"You should see the Mall of America," bragged Leland, as if he'd built it himself. "It makes this one look dinky."

When we weren't gawking, we spent our time getting used to the field, practicing running on Astro-Turf, which was like running on a huge welcome mat. It promised a nasty burn to anyone who fell with skin exposed. The VFW had sponsored a pancake feed to help us buy turf shoes.

It felt so good to be running again, limbs all oiled and ready to go—and to have some purpose. Every so often I snuck a look at the Dome's puffy ceiling, wondering if Young's angel might be hanging around.

That night, before we went to bed, Leland asked us if we wanted to pray with him. Leland was very religious, but not in a Jesus-freak way where he was pushing his religion on you. Jimmi rolled his eyes, but when he saw Mikko and me kneel down next to Leland, he grumbled and joined us.

Leland, like Coach, didn't pray for us to win, he just asked God to give us strength and stuff. I was almost jealous to see how much comfort he got from praying. He talked to God as if He were his uncle. I don't think I'd ever have the power to believe in something like that, something I couldn't see or touch.

"And we pray for Young, Chan's sister, may she watch over us also. Amen."

"Amen," I said. I opened my eyes. Mikko still had his eyes closed. Jimmi looked like he'd never shut his.

"It's been tough going, huh?" Leland asked.

"I miss her very much." I nodded over toward Mikko, who seemed to be trembling just the slightest bit.

"I think he does too."

forty

The Iron River contingent was very much in evidence. There were GO MINERS! banners spread across the stands, and a couple of the younger kids had painted their faces red and black, looking like they belonged in a deck of cards or something.

I looked into the stands until I found O-Ma, Abogee, and Mrs. Knutson. Their seats were in the middle of everything. All three of them were wearing Miners sweatshirts, even Abogee. They waved to me, Mrs. Knutson using her giant foam hand: WE'RE NUMBER ONE!

The coaches had needed to do some shuffling in order to tighten the lines in Rom's absence, but everyone seemed fine, ready to go. The band was playing happily in the comfort of climate control—no need to antifreeze the instruments. Big black cameras waited on the sidelines.

It was time for an extra point, yet another. Mikko caught the snap, and I could swear he was smiling under his helmet as he set it up. I was running loose and graceful, like a gazelle, and paced my way into the kick perfectly. My leg swung high in the air, long before any of the Seeyerville Heights players came near me.

That beautiful brown ball went sailing toward the stadium lights, which waited like stars.

My vision blurred from the brightness of the lights, and from a sound I heard.

"Did you hear that?" I yelled to Mikko. "Did you hear that, buddy?"

It was the pure, one-note cry of a flute.

forty-one

I am at the cemetery.

I walk over to the place where the earth is newly turned, where it swells up slightly, as if pregnant.

I brush off the headstone. My fingers are burned by the cold of the granite as I trace the grooves in the stone. YOUNG-BOON KIM, BELOVED DAUGHTER AND SISTER. REST IN PEACE.

Already, here, a red-and-black game jersey rests up against the stone. A teddy bear attached to it says SOMEONE IN THE MINNEAPPLE LOVES YOU.

I lean the trophy next to it. MINNESOTA STATE HIGH SCHOOL FOOTBALL CHAMPIONS. The gilded guy on the top is a kicker, just like me.

"I was going to burn it, Sis, but I thought it might melt. So here it is."

Some bits of white land on the back of my hand. Then more and more and more.

It is snowing. At least that's what I assume it is. I start to laugh, high-five the headstone.

"You see, Young?" I say as the falling snow blurs my vision. "It's your first snow! It's your first snow and your oppa is here to share it with you." I spread out my palms to catch the wafting flakes and am surprised to find they feel warm.

When I look up at the sky, it is gray and seems incredibly close, with a multitude of fat flakes whirling down. I want to spread my arms and go up to that place where the snow is coming from, but my feet stay planted, firmly, on the ground.

CONNECTIONS

Refugee Ship

Lorna Dee Cervantes

*Like Chan, the speaker in this poem has a troubled
relationship with the culture of her parents and grandparents. With her "bronzed skin" and "black hair," she
looks Hispanic but feels little connection to Hispanic culture. In this poem, the speaker talks about how it feels to
be trapped between her actual life and a cultural her-
itage that is not fully hers.*

Like wet cornstarch, I slide

past my grandmother's eyes. Bible

at her side, she removes her glasses.

The pudding thickens.

Mama raised me without language,

I'm orphaned from my Spanish name.

The words are foreign, stumbling

on my tongue. I see in the mirror

my reflection: bronzed skin, black hair.

I feel I am a captive

aboard the refugee ship.

The ship that will never dock.

El barco que nunca atraca.[1]

■   ■   ■

---

1. *El barco que nunca atraca:* The ship that never docks.

from *Children of the River*
Linda Crew

The novel Children of the River *tells the story of Sundara, a Cambodian girl who was forced, along with her aunt's family, to flee the political turmoil of her homeland. She was thirteen when she left Cambodia, leaving behind her parents and her brother and sister. Now, four years later, she is in high school, struggling to adjust to a still-strange culture and trying to please her aunt and uncle, who want her to remain a "good Cambodian girl."*

"So—how about it?" Jonathan said. "We could go to the movies if you want. Whatever."

"Oh . . ." She looked away from him, across the patio, stalling for time. A date. He was actually asking her out on a date. A picture flashed in her mind: Jonathan on the doorstep, like in the TV commercials, Naro and Soka looking him over, making him promise to bring her home on time. . . . No, no, never in a thousand years . . . She turned back to Jonathan. "Thank you, but I cannot."

"Come on, don't you like me?"

Her cheeks burned. "You teasing." He knew very well she liked him.

■■■■■■■■■■■■■■■■■■■■■■■■■■■■■■■■■■■■■

"Sorry." He smiled, not sorry at all. "But what's the problem?"

She bit her lip. "I like to go with you, but—in my country we don't go out on a date at all."

Still he smiled, refusing to take her seriously. "How do you figure out who you want to marry, then?"

"Our parents arrange. The boy's mother ask the girl's mother."

"But that's . . . *archaic*."

She lifted her chin. "My family would choose well for me. And my mother and father, they very happy together, even they see each other for the first time on their wedding day."

"Yeah?" He sounded skeptical.

She shifted away from him. "If the family make a good match, two people can grow to love each other. Our system not so bad." She gave him a side-long look. "In Cambodia we do not talk divorce every time somebody get mad."

"Hey, I didn't mean to sound critical. It's just that things are different here."

"Yes," she said, softening, "but not for me."

His smile had faded. He seemed bewildered. "So you really won't go out with me?"

"Jonatan, I shouldn't even have lunch with you. To go to the movie . . . I'm sorry. I just can't."

He blinked, at a loss. "Well . . . I guess if that's the way you feel . . ."

She thought about Cathy, about the other girls who gave him admiring glances. Perhaps no one had ever turned him down before. He looked so hurt.

But was she supposed to throw away the traditions of centuries to save the feelings of one American boy?

Of course not.

Still, imagine . . . to openly say to the world, *Yes, I want to be with him and he wants to be with me.* To venture into public, the two of them, alone together for all to see . . .

No, of course not.

But she couldn't pretend she hadn't felt it—a surprising little thrill of temptation.

In spite of her fears, Sundara found herself letting Jonathan fall in step beside her every day after international relations. Then she would follow him with her lunch tray to their special place on the patio. She watched herself doing this, day after day, almost as if she were watching someone else. So daring! Yet somehow the risk made her moments with Jonathan all the sweeter.

Then one day, when she had almost grown complacent, her luck ran out.

"I never understand why the American student so noisy in class," she was telling Jonathan as they finished their lunches. "Don't they want a good education?"

"Sure, I guess, but—"

"In my country, you get goofy like that—whap, whap—you gonna get it with a stick on your back!"

"They *beat* you?"

"Oh, yes. Or one teacher I have, he pinch your ear like this." She demonstrated, pretending to yank her gold earring.

"Sounds pretty rough."

"Well, they don't have to do that too much, because most of the student have good behavior. They know they must learn; they gonna be in big trouble at home if their parent find out they not respecting the teacher. But here . . ." She shook her head. "Even you! I'm shock when you get so sassy, ask so many question. Like yesterday in international relations when everybody argue? That make me kind of nervous."

"That was just a good discussion. Lanegren *wants* everyone to get involved."

"He like it when the student argue with him? In my country, you don't even dare ask the teacher to repeat if you don't understand. That like saying he doing a bad job of explaining. Same thing if somebody your boss."

"But if everybody's always pretending they understand when they don't, doesn't that lead to lots of misunderstandings?"

She frowned. "Sometime. But we don't like to argue about that face-to-face. We rather smooth it over, keep everything nice, try to understand without having a . . . what you call it?"

"A confrontation?"

"Yes! That the word. I'm shock when the American argue so much. Why you do this?"

"Beats me. I didn't know we did. Maybe we're just used to saying what we think."

"But sometime that so rude!"

He laughed. "Hey, Sundara, guess what?"

"What?"

"You're arguing!"

"Oh, you! You always make fun of—"

She stopped dead. Across the patio—Pok Simo with his Chinese friend. She held her breath, willing herself invisible. He hadn't seen her yet. But then his friend spotted her. He nudged Pok Simo.

Pok Simo took in their little scene—the lunch trays on the bench, the notebooks unopened. His eyes narrowed to a hard glare. She turned away, trembling. What fate! Of all people to walk by and find her alone with a white skin. For Pok Simo would love nothing better than to get her in trouble.

"You know him?" Jonathan asked.

She nodded, feeling sick. "He is Khmer also." Pok Simo resented the fact that her uncle had risen to the position of accountant while his father, once a high military attaché, now worked as a janitor. He resented even more Sundara's proud way of walking through the halls, her refusal to give him the deferential nod due one of high rank. Sundara shivered. He would savor his revenge in spreading this story.

"Is he gone yet?"

"Yeah, he took off. But what's his problem?"

She shook her head distractedly. Better if she had humbly bowed to Pok Simo each time they passed in the school halls, declaring herself lower than the dust beneath his feet. Now, for holding her head high, she would pay. Because what would Soka do if word of a white skin reached her ears?

News traveled fast among the Cambodians; Sundara did not expect to be kept in suspense long.

The following morning, her aunt's voice, harsher than usual, rudely ended Sundara's dream, a dream that somehow combined the warmth of Jonathan's smile with the softness of a night in Phnom Penh. Which was worse, the shattering nightmares, or waking from such loveliness at the snap of Soka's voice? Cold fear rushed through her as she remembered the previous day. Was it possible her aunt had already heard Pok Simo's story?

Sundara took her quick turn in the bathroom, washing her face, touching on some makeup, staring at her reflection. Did she look like a wicked girl? A girl who ate lunch alone with a boy? She would miss talking with him. Never before had anyone seemed so interested in her life, her feelings. What a relief it had been to speak of things so long held inside.

When she came into breakfast wearing jeans and a jade green blouse, Soka gave her one of those accusing looks. "You spend a lot of time on yourself lately."

Sundara swallowed. She *had* taken extra care in winding the ends of her hair around the curling iron, but her clothes were nothing special, except in comparison to Soka's. Soka refused to buy clothes for herself, and wished Sundara would also refrain. But Sundara didn't want to dress out of charity boxes as she'd had to at first. What fate! All those horrible pants suits of stretchy material . . . They were nothing like what the other girls were wearing. Not that she ever missed looking *exactly* like everyone else as she had at home, skipping to school each day in a blue skirt and white blouse. It was just that now she wanted to fit in with the Americans. She wanted jeans and tops like everyone else.

"Little ones! Come eat!" Soka had set their places to eat around the table western style. Now she poured the sugary cereal the boys had seen advertised on television.

Pon punched off his cartoons and carried in the jar of strawflowers he'd been wiring for Mr. Bonner's wife. He earned two cents for each stem he attached.

"Wonderful!" Soka said. "At least three dollars' worth. What a clever son." She gave his cheek a quick nuzzle. "Ravy, here is your note for the school."

"What's this?" Naro wanted to know as Ravy stuffed the paper in the back pocket of his jeans and sat down.

"The school called," Soka said. "They wanted me to write my permission so he can play football after school."

"Football? Ravy, why do you want to smash into other people?"

"It's flag football, Papa, not tackle. You just yank the flag out of the other guy's pocket."

Sundara and Ravy exchanged glances. She knew
very well he could hardly wait to play tackle.

"Talking to those people at his school is like
pouring water on a duck's back," Soka complained.
"No matter how many times I tell them, I cannot
make them understand that I am not Mrs. Tep,
there *is* no Mrs. Tep. I am Kem Soka, I tell them
on the phone yesterday, but it does no good."

"You should give up trying to put *Kem* first,"
Naro said. "It only confuses them."

She took a seat. "Well, I can understand that.
But why is it so difficult for them to understand a
married woman keeping the name she is born with?
They invented this women's lib, not us."

"Haven't you learned yet?" Naro said. "This is
their country. They don't care about our ways. We
are expected to imitate *them*."

"And some of their ways I don't mind. But I'll
tell you one thing, these children of ours must not
become too American." She took each of them in
with her eyes. "We don't want those bad things
happening to the children of *this* family. Drinking,
drugs, getting pregnant . . ."

Sundara's face got hot. She couldn't help it—
Soka's black eyes boring into her like that. If
her aunt's vague suspicions were this hard to

endure, imagine how terrifying to face her wrath at the truth!

Her cousins had gobbled their cereal and excused themselves. They went back down the hall to collect Ravy's homework papers and Pon's toy motorcycle for first grade show-and-tell.

"The best American idea, as far as I'm concerned," Soka went on, "is a man being allowed only one wife at a time." She gave Naro a pointed look, then turned back to Sundara. "At home Niece, if you get a good husband who makes a lot of money, there will always be younger women coming around, wanting to be wife number two. A terrible nuisance."

Sundara kept her eyes on her noodles, unable to enjoy the rare hint of intimacy in Soka's voice. Even if this old quarrel had lost its heat for Soka and Naro, it still served as an ominous reminder of her aunt's temper. To this day Sundara recalled overhearing her own parents discussing it—something about a younger woman, and Soka taking an ax to Naro's prized motorcycle. Sundara shuddered. Soka was not a good person to cross.

And how treacherously close Sundara always felt to Soka's anger. It was do this, don't do that, every minute of the day. Now that Soka had her food-service job at the university, she seemed to have completely forgotten how much she had depended on Sundara that first year, how much Sundara had helped her, answering the phone, going to the door while Soka cowered in the bedroom as if expecting to be dragged away. . . . For a while Sundara had hoped all this might win Soka's forgiveness for the baby's death,[1] but when Soka became strong again and unafraid, she also turned meaner than ever, as if blaming Sundara for her own period of helplessness.

Now her aunt spoke to Naro with excessive sweetness. "You're better off here, I think, where you can't talk to other women so much."

"You mean *you're* better off," he teased. "You know, you ought to watch how much *you* become American, Little Sister. You've put yourself high up enough in this family as it is."

"Too bad!" Soka replied, suppressing a smile, jutting her chin out at him.

"Oh Niece," Naro said with mock weariness, "why did my parents match me with such a sassy woman?"

---

1. When Sundara and her aunt and uncle fled Cambodia, Sundara was responsible for her aunt's newborn baby. Weakened by malnutrition, the baby soon died. Sundara's aunt is still mad at her for her failure to keep the baby alive.

Soka smiled broadly at this. She had good, even teeth, and a very nice look about her, Sundara thought, when she was joking with someone she liked. And they all knew Naro was only teasing, for Soka had proven a good wife to him. Especially after the first year in America, when he sank into depression. He, who had supported so many relatives at home, shamed by having to send his wife to work! But while he brooded in silence those long months, waiting for time to heal his spirit, Soka had been the most loyal and loving of wives.

Now he grinned at her. "At least she is better than the wife of Pok Sary." He jerked up his arms as if to ward off her blow.

"Ha! You *better* think so."

"I saw the two of them yesterday," he said. "Let me tell you, this is what *I* like about America: Here I don't have to bow down to *them*. You should have heard them, boasting about that son of theirs. It makes me tired."

Sundara's pulse raced at the mere mention of Pok Simo. Nervously she rose to fill her bowl again, hoping they wouldn't notice her hands shaking.

"You would think," Soka said, "that if they were so high-class they would have the good manners not to brag."

Naro nodded. "I've often thought that myself. I don't know how many times I've heard about their big brick house in Phnom Penh, their car, how everybody wanted to be their friend."

"I suppose we should try to be understanding," Soka said. "Perhaps we would feel the same way if we fell so low from so high up. But still . . ."

"Where's Grandmother?" Sundara said. "Not well again?"

Soka turned in her chair and gave Sundara one of those measuring looks. Had her attempt to change the subject been too obvious?

But to Sundara's relief, Soka merely sighed. "She doesn't want to eat. She doesn't even want to get out of bed today. Sometimes it seems hopeless. I finally persuade her to come to the supermarket with me, and then the checker is so rude Grandmother says she won't ever go back."

"They just don't have any respect for the elderly, do they?" Naro said. "And sometimes, Little Sister, I don't think *you* show her the respect she deserves, either."

"Me!" Soka was indignant. "What about you? You're not exactly humbling yourself for her advice all the time."

This stopped him. "Well, it's different here."

"Yes," she snapped, "I've noticed that." Then her voice softened. "I'm sorry, Naro. I do the best I can with your mother, but as you say, it's different here, and what can she tell us about coping with life in America when all she does is stay in the house, dreaming of home?"

"Ah, so understanding America is the way to be respected, then? If that's so, perhaps we should all fall on our knees before young Ravy!"

"Ha! Or Sundara here."

Oh, no. *How American Sundara Has Become.* A topic Soka relished and Sundara loathed. So unfair, to be criticized for everything right down to what Soka claimed was her overly bold way of walking. If only her aunt could see what an outsider she was at school. What did Soka think? That she could go to an American school and squat in the cafeteria to eat as if she were still half a world away? Would that have satisfied her? At home Sundara was too American; at school she felt painfully aware of not being American enough. She didn't fit in anywhere. *Please don't start on this,* she thought.

Fortunately, Soka seemed more inclined, at the moment, to analyze Grandmother's problems. "She has nothing like school or a job to force her out of the house. If only we could find something . . ." She considered this for a moment, then jumped up. "As for me, I have more than enough to do. That's the answer, you see. Work. Keep busy. Then there's less time to brood. Niece, you will start the dinner tonight so we can eat as soon as I get home. I promised to take that new family shopping for warm clothes tonight."

"They're having a sale at Valu-Time," Sundara offered, trying to be helpful. Unable to bargain here, Soka liked to at least find the best sales.

But Soka waved away that suggestion. "Last time I bought a jacket there the threads unraveled after one washing. I thought everything here would be good quality, but you really have to be careful."

Sundara nodded. The jacket she'd put on lay-away for herself was at one of the nice stores downtown. But Soka would consider that an extravagance, and would like it even less if she knew Sundara hadn't waited to walk in with cash. But after one more payday she'd have enough, and what if the beautiful plum-colored jacket were gone by then?

She scooped out the last of the noodles from the pot into her bowl, causing her aunt to cluck.

"That's your third bowl! I don't know why you're not fat, all the food you eat and nothing but sitting in school all day."

"I'm sorry," Sundara said meekly. "I should have asked if either of you would like the rest. Would you?"

Naro shook his head and Soka said she'd had enough—she was getting a bit plump herself lately—so Sundara ate the noodles. But Soka had spoiled her appetite.

Once out the door, Sundara began to breathe easier. Nothing said about Pok Simo. She sank into her bus seat thinking maybe she'd be lucky this time. Maybe they wouldn't find out. If she stayed away from Jonathan from now on, there was still a chance she might save herself.

And after all, was he really worth the risk? Maybe Cathy was right. Maybe she *was* just a curiosity to him. Maybe she was making a fool of herself, letting herself care about him as if there were the slightest chance they could ever belong to the same world.

Besides, she already had one failure on her conscience: the death of Soka's baby. There was no more room in her life for mistakes, large or small.

Yes, what she must do was quite clear. She would not think of him. She would not waste any more time looking for him in the halls. She would study hard during lunch hour the way she used to,

and when her parents came they would be proud.
She would not talk to him. She would not look at
him. She would forget it ever happened.

And then the school bus pulled up to the patio.
Through the tinted window, she saw him standing
by the flagpole. What was he doing there all by
himself? Usually she didn't see him until international
relations. He looked so nice. She loved those faded
jeans and that flannel shirt of his. The morning sun
shone on his blond hair as he tapped his notebook
against his thigh and looked around.

Her heart pounded, her knees felt weak as she
stood up in the bus aisle. She must pretend she
hadn't seen him and walk past to the building.
With so many students milling around, maybe she'd
escape his notice.

But when she stepped off the bus, he hurried
right toward her. He had been waiting especially for
her. He knew which bus she rode.

"Sundara! I've got to talk to you." He led her
away from the others. His hand on her arm felt nice,
nicer than it should have. "How about explaining that
little scene yesterday. Is that guy your boyfriend or
something?"

She glanced up at him in surprise. "Oh, no! He
be mad to hear you say this. We not the same class."

"So? Lots of girls go out with older guys. I thought—"

"Not class in school! *Social class,* don't you know? Oh, too hard to explain now." She looked over her shoulder. Were they being watched?

"But why'd you run off, then?"

"Because he *see* us. With my people everyone watch everyone else. He will talk."

"We were just sitting there."

"But I am a girl and you are a boy!"

"You noticed that too, huh?"

"Oh, you make fun!" Her voice wavered between a giggle and a wail; her cheeks were warm. "I could get in trouble. How many times do I have to tell you? In Cambodia a girl doesn't go with a boy alone."

"You're in America now."

"Oh, is that so?" She made a face. "Sometime I forget!"

He grinned. "Meet me for lunch?"

"*Jonatan.*" So persistent! Was it possible he really didn't understand? How blunt you sometimes had to be with Americans! But the longer she stayed there with him in the fresh morning air, the easier it was to let herself be persuaded, the harder it was to tell him they must not see each other. Soka had a strong power over her, but so did Jonathan.

And right now, as he stood looking at her with those strange and lovely blue eyes, she just *liked* him, liked the way he made her feel, liked the way he was banishing her nightmares by stealing into her dreams. Was that so terrible? After all, it was not as if staying away from him would bring the baby back to life. . . .

"Okay," she said. "I meet you." And her heart beat with the most extraordinary mixture of joy and fear.

■ ■ ■

Stealing for Girls
Will Weaver

Chan and the main character of this short story, Sun, have one big thing in common: They're both struggling for acceptance. Chan struggles to be accepted by his high school football team. Sun's struggle, however, is much closer to home: She simply wants her father to accept her as a daughter and *an athlete, an acceptance her little brother has without question.*

It's a free country right? I choose my clothes (sixties retro), I choose my shoes (Nikes), I choose my CDs (Hendrix and Nine Inch Nails), I choose my friends (you know who you are). If I were an adult (which I'm not—I'm a fourteen-year-old eighth-grade girl named Sun) I could vote, could choose my car, my career, whatever—like I said, a free country, right?

Wrong.

Quiz time: Please take out a number two lead pencil; *do not* open the test booklet until you're told. Seriously, my question to you is this: What's the most majorly thing in your life that you *can't* choose?

The answer is as simple as the eyes and nose on your face: your parents. Your parents and your brothers or sisters. That's because no matter how free you think you are, the only thing nobody can choose for herself is her own family.

Here's another way of putting it: Being born is something like arriving at a restaurant where there are no waitrons[1] and no menus. Your table is set and your food is there waiting for you. It might be fresh shrimp, it might be steak, it might be macaroni hot dish, it might be all broccoli; for some kids there might be no food at all, maybe not even a table.

Me? I was fairly lucky. My parents are (1) there, and (2) at least semicool most of the time. My dad's an accountant and my mom's a college professor. Both are in their middle forties, physically fit, and usually unembarrassing in public. My gripe is the old basic one for girls: My father spends way more time on sports with my brother, Luke, than with me.

Luke is in sixth grade, is already taller than me, and can pound me at basketball. At Ping-Pong. At any sport. You name it, he crushes me. I want to say right here I'm not a klutz. I'm nearly five feet six

---

1. *Waitrons:* Gender-neutral term for both waiters and waitresses

and have at least average coordination; on our basketball team I'm third off the bench, which is not that shabby considering that our school, Hawk Bend, is a basketball power in central Minnesota. But I won't play one-on-one with Luke anymore. No way. Who likes to lose every time? It's not like he's mean or wants to humiliate me—he's actually pretty decent for a twerpy sixth-grade boy—it's just that he's a natural athlete and I'm not.

I am thinking these thoughts as I sit next to my parents watching Luke's team play Wheatville. Luke just made a nifty spin move (of course, he's the starting point guard) and drove the lane for a layup. My mother, who comes to most games, stares at Luke with her usual astounded look. She murmurs to my father, who comes to all our games, "How did he *do* that?"

"Head fake right, plant pivot foot, big swing with leading leg, and bingo—he's by," my dad whispers. A quiet but intense man with salt-and-pepper hair, he speaks from the side of his mouth, for there are always parents of other sixth-graders nearby.

"He amazes me," my mother says. She has not taken her eyes off Luke. I hate to agree, but she's right—all of which clouds further my normally

■■

"sunny" disposition. I remember Dad and Luke working last winter on that very move in the basement; I went downstairs to see what was going on, and they both looked up at me like I was an alien from the *Weekly World News.* My father soon enough bounced the ball to me, and I gave it a try, but I could never get my spin dribble to rotate quickly enough and in a straight line forward to the basket. Not like you-know-who. "Watch Luke," my father said. "He'll demonstrate."

Now, at least it's the third quarter of the game and Luke already has a lot of points and his team is ahead by twenty so the coach will take him out soon—though not quite soon enough for Wheatville, or me. At the other end of the court Luke's loose, skinny-legged body and flopping yellow hair darts forward like a stroke of heat lightning to deflect the ball.

"Go, Luke!" my father says, half rising from his seat.

Luke is already gone, gathering up the ball on a break-away, finishing with a soft layup high off the board. People clap wildly.

I clap slowly. Briefly. Politely. My mother just shakes her head. "How does he *do* that?"

"Ask *him*," I mutter.

"Pardon, Sun?" my mom says abstractedly.

"Nothing." I check the scoreboard, then my own watch. I've seen enough. Below, at floor level, some friends are passing. "I think I'll go hang with Tara and Rochelle," I say to my parents.

"Sure," my mother says vacantly.

Dad doesn't hear me or see me leave.

As I clump down the bleachers there is more cheering, but I prefer not to look. "Sun." What a stupid name—and by the way I do not *ever* answer to "Sunny." I was allegedly born on a Sunday, on a day when the sun was particularly bright, or so my parents maintain. I seriously doubt their version (someday I'm going to look up the actual weather report on March 18, 1980). I'm sure it was a Monday; either that or I was switched at the hospital. Or maybe it was Luke—one of us, definitely, was switched.

Rochelle, actually looking once or twice at the game, says right off, "Say wasn't that your little brother?"

"I have no brother," I mutter.

"He's a smooth little dude," Tara says, glancing over her shoulder. "Kinda cute, actually."

"Can I have some popcorn or what?" I say.

"Or what," Rochelle says, covering her bag.

They giggle hysterically. Real comediennes, these two.

"When's your next game?" Tara says to me, relenting, giving me three whole kernels.

"The last one is Tuesday night," I answer. "A makeup game with Big Falls."

"Here or away?"

"Here."

"With your record, maybe you could get your little brother to play for your team."

"Yeah—a little eye shadow, a training bra," adds Rochelle, "everyone would think he was you!"

I growl something unprintable to my friends and go buy my own bag of popcorn.

*   *   *

At supper that night Luke and I stare at each other during grace, our usual game—see who will blink first. Tonight it is me. I glare down at my broccoli and fish; I can feel him grinning.

"And thank you, God, for bouncing the ball our way once again," my father finishes. "Amen." If God doesn't understand sports metaphors, our family is in huge trouble.

"Well," my father says, looking at Luke expectantly.

"A deep subject," Luke says automatically, reaching for his milk, automatically.

Both of them are trying not to be the first one to talk about the game.

"How was your day, Sun?" my mother says.

"I hate it when you do that."

"Do what?" my mother says.

"It's condescending," I add.

"What is condescending?" she protests.

"Asking me about my day when the thing on everybody's mind is Luke's usual great game. Why not just say it: 'So Luke, what were the numbers?'"

There is silence; I see Luke cast an uncertain glance toward my father.

"That's not at all what I meant," Mother says.

"And watch that tone of voice," my father warns me.

"So how many points *did* you get?" I say to Luke, clanking the broccoli spoon back into the dish, holding the dish in front of his face; he hates broccoli.

He shrugs, mumbles, "Not sure, really."

"How many?" I press.

"I dunno. Fifteen or so." But he can't help himself: He bites his lip, tries to scowl, fakes a cough, but the smile is too strong.

"How *many?*" I demand.

"Maybe it was twenty," he murmurs.

I pick up a large clump of broccoli and aim it at his head.

"Sun!" my father exclaims.

Luke's eyes widen. "Twenty-six!" he squeaks.

"There. That wasn't so difficult, was it?" I say, biting the head off the broccoli.

Luke lets out a breath, begins to eat. There is a silence for a while.

"By the way—nice steal there at the end," I say to him as I pass the fish to Father.

Luke looks up at me from the top of his eyes. "Thanks," he says warily.

"It's something I should work on," I add.

"I'll help you!" Luke says instantly and sincerely. "Right after supper!"

At this syrupy sibling exchange, my parents relax and dinner proceeds smoothly.

Later, during dessert, when my father and Luke have finally debriefed themselves—quarter by quarter, play by play—on the game, I wait for Dad's

....

usual "Well, who's next on the schedule, Luke?"
He doesn't disappoint me.

"Clearville, I think," Luke says.

"Any breakdown on them? Stats?"

"They're eight-four on the season, have that big
center who puts up *numbers,* plus a smooth point
guard. They beat us by six last time," Luke says.
My mind skips ahead twenty years and sees Luke
with his own accounting office, crunching tax
returns by day and shooting hoops long into the
evening.

"Big game, then, yes?" my father remarks, his
fingers beginning to drum on the table. "You'll have
to box out—keep that big guy off the boards. And if
their point guard penetrates, collapse inside—make
him prove he can hit the jumper."

"He can't hit no jumpers," Luke says through a
large bite of cake. "He shoots bricks, and I'm going
to shut him down like a bike lock."

"Huh?" I say.

"What?" Luke says. "What'd I say now?"

"First off, it's 'any jumper.' And second, how do
you shut someone down 'like a bike lock'?"

"Actually, it's not a bad simile," my mother
says. "If this fellow is 'smooth,' so, in a way, is a

bicycle—they way it rolls and turns—and a bike lock, well . . ." She trails off, looking at me.

I shrug and stare down at my fish. It has not been a good day for either of us.

"And who does *your* team play next, Sun?" my father asks dutifully.

"Big Falls. Tuesday night," I say. I look up and watch his face carefully. "Tuesday night, isn't that? . . ." he begins.

"I'm afraid I'll miss it, honey," my mother interjects. "I have that teachers' education conference in Minneapolis, remember?"

"Sure, Mom, no problem." I keep my eyes on my father; on Luke, who's thinking. I am waiting for the lightbulb (twenty watts, maximum) to go on in his brain.

"Hey—Tuesday night is my game, too," Luke says suddenly.

"Yes, I thought so," my father murmurs. The one-on-one experts have finally put two and two together.

"What time are your games?" my mother asks.

"Seven," Luke and I say simultaneously.

My father looks to me, then to Luke. He's frowning. Suddenly his gaze lightens. "By any chance are they both at the high school? In the adjoining gyms?"

"Middle school," Luke says.

"High school," I follow.

"Damn," my father says, "they ought to take whoever schedules sporting events in this school system and—"

"I'm sure it couldn't be helped, dear," my mother interjects. "Sun's is a makeup game, after all."

"And the last one of the season," I add.

My father looks to Luke. "So is yours, right? The last one of the season?"

Luke nods. He and I look at each other. I smile. I love moral dilemmas, especially when they're not mine.

My father turns to my mother.

"Sorry," she says to him, "I'm delivering a speech in Minneapolis. There's no way I can miss it."

"Well," my father says, drumming his fingers, "I'll have to think this one through."

*   *   *

Amazingly, Luke keeps his promise, and after dinner we work on stealing. It is chilly outside in

■■■■■■■■■■■■■■■■■■■■■■■■■■■■■■■■■

March, with patches of leftover snowbanks along the north side of the garage (this is Minnesota, remember), but the asphalt is clear.

"There are two main types of steals," Luke says, dribbling. "First is the most basic, 'the unprotected ball.' As your man is dribbling, he is not shielding the ball with his body, and so you go for it."

"I have part of a brain," I say, and lunge for the deflection—but Luke instantly back-dribbles, and I miss.

"It's all in the timing," he says, "all in when you start your move. Don't start when the ball is coming back up to my hand—begin your move just when the ball *leaves* my hand, just when it's released and heading downward."

I track him, waiting—then try it. This time I actually knock the ball away.

"See?" Luke says. "That gives you the maximum time for your reach-in."

We practice this a few more times.

"Be sure to reach with your outside hand," Luke cautions, "or else you might get called for a reach-in foul."

We keep working for quite a while. I start to get every third one, but I'm still not very good at it.

"It's coming," Luke says, then holds the ball. I kick away a pebble, which clatters against the garage door.

"The second type of steal is called the wrap-around. It's when your man is dribbling and you reach way around behind, almost wrapping your arm around him, and knock the ball away." He flips me the ball, has me dribble, and snakes loose the ball two out of three times. Then he takes the ball back, and we work on this one for a while. I get one out of ten at best. Soon I am panting.

"The wraparound is the toughest one," Luke says. "Maybe you need longer arms or something."

From the window, my father is watching us. "Again," I say crabbily to Luke. Soon I am stumbling-tired and getting no wraparound deflections or steals at all.

"Hey—it'll come," Luke says, bouncing the ball to me. I slam the ball hard onto the cold asphalt and back into my hands.

"Yeah. Like in 2010 maybe," I say, then mutter something unprintable.

"Ah . . . I think I'll go have some more cake," Luke says.

"Fine!" I bark. He heads off.

"By the way," I call after him, "who taught you those stealing moves?" The middle-school coaches teach both the girls' and boys' teams, and I am always on the lookout for coaches who treat boys and girls differently. Nothing pisses me off more than that.

"Who taught me? Coach Dad," Luke says with an innocent smile.

I don't smile. I glare at Luke, then to the window, which is empty.

"What?" Luke says, glancing behind. "What did I say now?"

"Nothing." I turn away, take the ball, and begin to bank hard shots off the backboard, none of which fall.

* * *

That night, as my father sits at the kitchen table rattling his calculator keys and turning the pages of someone's tax return (from March through April 15 we leave him alone), I find myself rattling the dishes hard and loud as I clean up the kitchen.

"Was there something? . . ." he says irritatedly, glancing up only briefly from his papers.

"No," I say, and stomp past him upstairs to my room.

▪▪▪

Later I hear my mother speaking softly to my father. He lets out a sigh and pushes back from the table. Soon I hear his footsteps on the stairs, and then he pops his head partway into my room, where I am reading. "Everything okay, Sun?"

"Sure," I mutter.

"Sure sure?"

I shrug.

He leans in my doorway. "So what is it?" he asks, checking his watch.

"How come you taught Luke those two types of steals and not me?" I turn to him. My eyes, disgustingly, feel glassy and spilly; they are about to dump water down my cheeks.

He stares. "Steals? Oh, you mean . . . Yes, well . . ." He trails off and stares at some empty space in front of him, thinking. Then he turns to me. "I guess I just naturally do more sports stuff with Luke because . . . because we're both boys—I mean I once was, and he's one now, that sort of thing," he finishes lamely.

"Well, I play basketball, too, dammit!" I say. I try to be hard-boiled but a large tear rolls down my cheek. "Damn," I blurt, and start crying for real.

He stares at me, then moves imperceptibly, as if to come forward either to smack me for swearing or

to take me in his arms. But accountants are accountants because most of them are not good with other
things—like feelings. With a confused look on his
face, my father retreats from my room.

In the morning when I wake up, there is a note
taped to my door. In his small, careful handwriting
my father has written, "Dear Sun: There is a third
type of steal. . . ."

* * *

That Saturday, when Luke is gone to hockey, my
father appears in the TV room wearing his tennis shoes
and sweats. "'Stealing for Girls,' a sports clinic by
yours truly, begins in fifteen minutes, garage-side."

I smile, grab the remote, and shoot the TV dead.

Before we go outside, my father sits at the
kitchen table and begins drawing neat *X*'s and *O*'s on
graph paper. "We'll call this third type the prediction
pass steal. It's something that works best with a zone
defense."

"Okay," I say. On my team we have been learning the zone, and zone traps, though we haven't
used them much.

"A half-court zone defense forces the team on
offense to work the ball around the perimeter."

I nod as he draws lines in a large half circle.

"The faster the ball movement, the tougher it is for the defense to shift accordingly."

I nod. I know all this.

"The offensive point guard will sooner or later get into what you might call the automatic pass mode—he receives a pass from, say, his right side, and automatically turns to pass his left."

"Yeah, sure," I murmur, for I am thinking of something that has always puzzled me.

"What is it?" my father asks with a trace of impatience.

"If you never played basketball in high school or college, how come you know so much about the game?"

He looks up straight at me. There is a long moment of silence. "I would like to have played," he says simply, "but it was a big school."

I meet his gaze, then put my hand on his shoulder.

He smiles, a small but real smile, and we both turn back to the graph paper.

"Anyway, when the point guard gets sloppy," he continues, "that's when the smart defensive man can start to think about a prediction pass steal."

"The defensive point guard?"

"No," my father says immediately. "The offensive point guard is used to that; he's been conditioned to watch out for that kind of steal. What he's not expecting is the weak-side defensive guard or even the forward to break up and across, slanting through the lane toward the key and picking off the pass. A lot of the quick but small college teams use it."

"Show me," I say, staring down at the paper.

He grabs a fresh graph. "Imagine a basic zone defense that's shifting to the ball."

I close my eyes. "Got it," I say.

"If the offense is moving the ball sharply, the defensive point guard has the toughest job. He usually can't keep up with the ball movement."

I nod. I keep my eyes closed.

"So the passes out front become 'gimmes'; they're not contested."

I nod again.

"And after a while, the offensive point guard gets sloppy. That's when one of the defensive players down low—the forward or center—can make his move. He flashes all the way up, comes out of nowhere for the steal."

My smile opens my eyes.

"Keep in mind it will only work once or twice," my father cautions, "and the timing has to be perfect—or the defense will get burned."

I look down to his drawing, see the open hole left by the steal attempt.

"Burned bad," he adds. "But if it works— bingo—he's gone for an easy layup."

I correct him: *"She's* gone."

* * *

Outside, for want of five offensive players, my father presses into service a sawhorse, three garbage cans, and my mother. "I just love my team," she says wryly.

"This won't take long," my dad says. Mom shivers; the weather is cloudy, with rain forecast.

"Sun, you're the weak-side defensive guard," he directs. I position myself, back to the basket. "Honey, you're our offensive point guard," he says to my mother.

"I've never been a point guard; I've never been a guard of any kind," she protests.

"First time for everything," my dad retorts.

Actually, I can tell that they're both having at least a little fun.

"Now," he says to my mom, "imagine you have just received a pass from the sawhorse, and in turn you'll be passing to me."

My mother, the orange ball looking very large in her hands, says, "Thanks—sawhorse," and turns and passes to my dad.

"Now—Sun!" he calls, but I break up way too late. "Again," my father says.

This time I break up too soon, and my mother stops her pass.

"Again," my father says.

I trot back to my position and try it again. On the sixth try I time it perfectly: I catch her pass chest-high and am gone for an imaginary layup.

"Excellent!" my father calls. "Again."

We practice until we are glowing in the chilly March morning, until an icy rain starts spattering down and the ball becomes too slick to hold.

Afterward, we are sitting at the kitchen table drinking hot chocolate when outside a car door slams—Luke's ride—and then Luke thumps into the house. "Hey," he says, pointing over his shoulder, "what's with the garbage cans and the sawhorse?"

The three of us look at each other; I smile and say nothing.

* * *

For the next several days, my father and I work exactly forty-five minutes per evening on the prediction pass steal. I let Luke join us only because we need another passer. The weather remains lousy, and my mother freezes her butt off, and Luke complains about not getting to try the prediction steal himself, but my father ignores all that. He is too busy fine-tuning my timing, my breakaways.

And, suddenly, it is Tuesday morning of game day. Both games.

"Huge day—two big games," my father says, first thing, at breakfast. He drums his fingers, glances at his briefcase, at the clock.

Luke glares at me. He is not happy about this week and his role as perpetual passer. "I guess I know which game *you're* going to," He mutters to my father.

My father says nothing.

* * *

Warming up with the team, I have the usual butterflies. The Big Falls girls look like their name—big, with huge hair tied back and bouncing like waterfalls as they do their layups. I try not to look at them, but can't help but hear their chatter, the chirp and thud of their shoes. Even their feet are huge.

I look around the gym. No family. No Dad. I miss my layup.

Just before tip-off, from my spot on the bench, I look around one last time. No family. No father. I sigh and try to focus on the game.

* * *

During the halftime shoot I scan the crowd. Still nobody. I feel something inside me harden further, and center itself; it's a flash of what life will be like when I go away to college, when I'll truly be on my own. Just me. No family whatsoever. Just me shlumping along through life.

On the bench as the third quarter begins, for some reason I finally get focused. I sit next to the coach; I chatter out encouragement. Our fast break begins to work. After they score or we get a rebound, Rachel rips the ball to one side or the other while Jenny, our point guard, breaks up the center. She takes the pass at the half-court line, then does her thing—either driving the lane or dishing off to the trailers. We miss some easy layups but still pull within one point.

Big Falls calls time-out. Our subs are ecstatic, but the starting five stand bent over, hands on knees, wheezing.

"Let's try to keep the fast break working through the end of this quarter," Coach Brown says, "and then we'll figure out something else."

Our starters manage a weak "Go Fliers" and trudge back onto the floor.

In the final two minutes of the third quarter I watch as Big Falls shuts down the fast break like . . . like a bicycle lock. Simple, really—just some pressure on the out-of-bounds first pass, plus coverage on the sides—and we do not score again. But I have been watching them on offense. Nearly every time down the court, Pimple Shoulders rears up inside, then looks for the pass from the point guard—who has taken very few shots from the perimeter, including zero three-point attempts.

"Zone," I say to myself. "In the fourth quarter we should go zone."

Coach Brown looks to me. Then back to the action. He strokes his chin.

At the final quarter break he kneels on the floor. "Take a load off," he commands, and the starting five slump into chairs. He points, one by one, to the next five, and we check in. Back in the huddle, Coach Brown has drawn some scrawling maps of *X*'s and *O*'s. "Zone defense," he says, with a wink to me. "Let's collapse inside and make them shoot from the perimeter. Make them prove they can hit the jumpers. But box out and get that rebound," he adds. "We've got to have the ball to score."

We fire up and trot onto the floor. For some reason I look to the middle of the bleachers—and see my father. His briefcase rests beside him and his gray suit coat is folded neatly over it.

"Zone! Box and one!" the Big Falls point guard calls out immediately, and begins to move the ball crisply side to front to side. It's clear they've had a zone thrown at them before. Still bench-stiff, we have trouble keeping up with the passes, and their point guard takes an uncontested shot from within the key—but bricks it. Wendy rips off the rebound and we move the ball cautiously upcourt. Our second-team guards have no future with the Harlem Globetrotters in terms of ballhandling, but we do know how to pick-and-roll.

I fake to the baseline, then break up and set a screen for Shanna. She rubs off her girl—who hits me, blindside, hard—as I roll to the inside. I'm looking for the ball, and suddenly, thanks to a nifty bounce pass, it's right at my chest. I clamp on it, take one dribble, brace for a hammer blow from Pimple Shoulders, and go up for the lay-in. I feel the oncoming air rush of a large-body (the image of a 747 jetliner on a crash course with a seagull flashes through my mind) but don't alter my flight path. The ball feels good off my fingertips. As my feet touch down and I open my eyes, the ball is settling through the net and Pimple Shoulders is skidding along the hardwood runway and there is major cheering from our bench. Me? I am just happy to be heading up court with all my feathers intact.

The Big Falls outside shooting continues to bang hard off the rim, and we continue to box out and get the rebound play and score on basic pick-and-rolls. We go up 42–38, and our bench is screaming and bouncing up and down in their chairs.

But Big Falls gets smart: They throw a zone defense at us. Not great passers, and worse outside shooters, we turn the ball over three times; barely fifty seconds later, Big Falls is up by two, 44–42, and Coach Brown is screaming for a time-out. By the time the ref stops the clock there is less than three minutes left in the game.

• •

"Okay, good job, second team," He calls, pointing for the first team to check back in. "Stay with the zone defense, but let's run the fast break."

We all clap once, together, and send the starters back onto the floor.

"Nice work out there," the coach says to me and motions for me to sit by him. "Stay ready."

The first team, refreshed, runs a fast break for a quick bucket and knots the score at 44 all. The teams trade baskets, then settle into solid defense, and suddenly there is less than one minute to play. Both the score and my gut are knotted. The Big Falls point guard launches a three-pointer, which goes through, but we come back with a fast break on which Rachel does some kind of wild, falling, 180-degree, dipsy-do finger-roll shot—which falls! We are down by one point, but Rachel is down, too, with a turned ankle. There are thirty seconds left.

We help her off the court. Done for the day, she cries with pain and anger.

"Sun—check in and go to forward," the coach says.

As I pause at the scorer's table, everything seems exaggeratedly clear, as if magnified: the black and white zebra stripes of the officials, the

seams of the yellow wood floor, the orange rim
worn to bare, shiny metal on the inside. I stare at
the ball the ref is holding and can imagine its warm,
tight sphere in my hands. I want that ball. For the
first time in my basketball career I want the ball, bad.

The Big Falls girls are slapping high fives like
the game is over; after all, they have possession
with a one-point lead. The ref calls time-in, and Big
Falls bounces the ball inbounds handily and pushes
it quickly up the floor. There they spread the offense
and begin to work the ball around the perimeter:
side to front to side to front. It's too early for us to
foul, so we stay with our zone defense. Their point
guard, still jazzed from making the three-point basket is loose and smart-mouthed. As she receives the
ball she automatically passes it to the opposite side.

Which is when I suddenly see not Big Falls
players but garbage cans and a sawhorse. To the
side, on the bench, I see Coach Brown rising to
signal it's time to foul, but I have been counting off
another kind of time: the Big Falls passing rhythm.
On the far side, away from the ball, when orange
is flashing halfway to the point guard, I begin my
break. Smart Mouth receives the ball, turns, and
passes it. Her eyes bug out as I arrow into view;

she tries to halt her pass but it's too late. I catch the ball and am gone. There is only open floor in front and sudden cheering from the sides, and, overly excited, I launch my layup at about the free throw line—but the ball goes in anyway. The Hawk Bend crowd goes crazy.

Down by one point, Big Falls calls a frantic time-out at the five-second mark. Our players are delirious, but Coach Brown is not. "Watch for the long pass, the long pass!" he rants. "They have a set play. Don't foul—especially on the three-point shot."

But we're only eighth-graders; at times we don't listen well.

Sure enough, Big Falls screens on the inbound pass, which Pimple Shoulders fires full court. There the point guard takes an off-balance shot—and is fouled by Shanna as time runs out.

Shanna looks paralyzed. She can't believe she did it.

"Three-point attempt—three foul shots!" the ref calls.

We clear off the free throw line and watch her make the first two—to tie—and miss the third. The game goes into overtime.

Back in the huddle we try to get pumped again, but I can tell it's not going to happen. We are stunned and flat. We lose in overtime by four points.

*   *   *

Back home we have a late supper: broccoli, fish sticks, and rice. I stare at my plate as my father finishes grace. Then he looks up. "Well," he says.

"A very deep subject," Luke replies, grabbing the bread. His team won, of course, by twenty-six points.

I just sit there, slumped and staring.

"You should have seen it," my father begins, speaking to Luke. "We're down by one and your sister is low on the weak side. The Big Falls point guard is not paying attention. . . ." Slowly I look up. I listen as my father tells the story of my one and only career steal. He re-creates it so well that Luke stops eating and his mouth drops open slightly. "Rad!" Luke says at the finish, then asks me more about my game. I shrug, but end up giving him a virtual play-by-play of the last two minutes.

When I am done, Luke lets out a breath and looks squarely at me. "Wow—I wish I could have been there!"

I stop to stare at him.

"What—what'd I say?" Luke says warily.

I just smile, and pass my little brother the broccoli.

■ ■ ■

Success Saga in America: Korean Style

Elizabeth Mehren

From the *Los Angeles Times*

This newspaper article tells the story of a man very similar to Chan's father, Abogee. Like Abogee, Chung U Chon left Korea to start a new life in America. Although this article was written in 1987, his story still captures the essence of many Korean immigrants' experience in America.

As a boy in Korea, Chung U Chon dreamed of the good life, the life he knew he would find in America. He dreamed of big houses, cars, an important job and many people working for him. Someday, he told his parents and his six brothers, he would move to America and make that dream a reality.

The day he moved his wife and three children into their $75-a-month, fifth-floor walkup apartment in Brooklyn 11 years ago, that dream played over and over in Chung's head. There was no hot water, and only a large vat to bathe in. The walls were filthy, and at any moment, the ceiling threatened a cave-in.

Chung's wife, Sun, burst into tears. "You made us sell our house in Korea for this?" she accused him. "For this life?"

Late that night, when Chung finally prepared to fall asleep, mice scampered across the pillow.

Now, surveying his corner kingdom in Manhattan's Washington Heights neighborhood, greengrocer Chung can smile at the irony of those memories.

His days still begin with a trip to the big wholesale produce center in the Bronx at 3:30 A.M., and each day Chung is still in his store, the California Fruit Market, when it closes at 7 o'clock at night.

But now Chung oversees six employees. From the 18-hour days she worked when they first entered the produce business, his wife has cut back to a less grueling schedule, sometimes even taking days off at midweek. They have a four-bedroom house in Norwood, N.J., and an assortment of shiny cars. Two children are in college; the third recently completed nursing school. Chung, 49, has become an American citizen. Not long ago, he took up golf.

These days Chung presides over a lush cornucopia lining the sidewalk at 183rd Street and St. Nicholas Avenue: corn, cucumbers, cabbage, beets, broccoli, bananas—his inventory reads like the produce section in Eden.

Pausing one recent morning after straightening a box of nectarines, Chung tossed a peach in the air, caught it, and bit into it with wicked delight. From under his blue baseball cap, a grin spread across his face.

"In this country, you still got a lot of chances," Chung said. "You want to make money here, you can make money. You can do anything in this country."

Then he added what might have been an endorsement for the ethic on which America was founded.

"If you work hard," he said. "Work *very* hard."

In New York, the prospect of round-the-clock shifts selling foodstuffs that are often foreign to their own culture has not deterred thousands of Chung's countrymen from taking over the leases of small groceries and delicatessens that fall idle with an owner's death or retirement.

In the space of a decade, at least 1,300 such stores in New York's five boroughs have been turned over to Korean ownership. All around the city, entire families of Koreans make tending them a group experience: Grandmother on the sidewalk, peeling vegetables for the salad bar; wife at the cash register; husband loading boxes; children straightening the displays; grandfather watching over the buckets of flowers. In Manhattan, "the Koreans'" has come to be the short name for the corner fruit-and-vegetable store.

Almost no one spoke Korean when Chung U Chon began haunting the Bronx's wholesale produce center 11 years ago. His own English was so shaky then, and his familiarity with American taste in produce so limited, that he had friends write down the names of particular items in English so he could show the list to the wholesalers.

"Navel oranges," he said. "I never knew there was more than one kind of orange. Peppers. I never knew there were so many varieties."

Now Chung estimates that 70% of the merchants who pull up to the warehouses at 3 and 3:30 in the morning are Koreans. "All around you, what you hear spoken is Korean," he said.

New Korean immigrants gravitated to the fruit and vegetable business because they are "labor-oriented and very hard-working," Eugene Kang, executive director of the Korean Produce Assn. Inc., said.

"Before the Korean immigrants landed in this city, who were the greengrocers?" Kang asked. "Most likely, they were Jewish and Italian, along with Greeks."

But those ethnic groups fell prey to the third-generation syndrome, Kang said, where sons-of-sons of immigrants were not willing to labor long hours in a business decidedly lacking in glamour.

"The Jews and Italians and Greeks, they are third generation now," Kang said. "They want to go to law school. They are no longer taking care of father's business, which was greengrocer."

Like Chung U Chon, many of the Koreans who set up as greengrocers are college-educated. As Chung did in 1974, they often arrive carrying their life's savings, sometimes tens of thousands of dollars or more. Because so many Korean emigrants send generous amounts of money to their relatives at home, South Korea's government encourages the tide of its citizens to this country by offering free language lessons, job training and orientation programs.

Coming to America

For Chung, no such opportunities existed when he uprooted his family and headed to the United States. Once a language student at the University of Seoul, he had supplanted his schoolboy's English by palling around with GIs in Korea. But Sun spoke no English, not one word.

Chung first chose to settle in Washington, where he had friends. Having worked in hotel management in Korea, he quickly landed a job at Washington's Statler Hilton Hotel, earning "$160, $170 a week,

■■■■■■■■■■■■■■■■■■■■■■■■■■■■■■■■■■■■

about the same as in Korea." Sun, a housewife in Korea, went to work as a busgirl in a cafeteria in the mornings, and as a housemaid in the afternoons, earning half as much.

Expenses were high. They had to buy a car, and rent, clothes and food cost far more than they had expected.

"We thought it would be cheaper here," Chung said. "But surprise, much more expensive."

In a year and a half they watched the $20,000 life's savings they had brought from Korea dwindle to $6,000.

Panicked, Chung flew to California to visit a Korean friend who had a 7-Eleven franchise in San Jose. The whole family worked in the store, his friend told him, spreading their shifts through the day. Chung was impressed; he submitted his own application for a California fast-food-store franchise.

But on a last-minute whim after he returned to Washington, Chung decided that before he left, he wanted to see New York. One Sunday, he and a friend climbed in the car and headed up Route 95.

"We came out the Holland Tunnel, right into Chinatown," Chung said, eyes widening at the recollection. Chung thought he was home at last. "It looked just like Seoul at that time."

In 24 hours, Chung changed his mind. He would move the family to New York, not California.

"All the people here, in New York, they told me it was better here than in California," he said. "They said you don't need a car, they got a subway. Apartments are cheap. You can take the bus. All this kind of story I hear from people here."

Yet another Korean friend knew a woman who wanted to sell her corner fruit-and-vegetable store in Brooklyn. Chung negotiated, and for $5,000, the place was his.

"I didn't look around, I didn't know where was Brooklyn, where was Manhattan, where was the highway," Chung said.

"I felt like I had no more chances, like 'this is it. This is my last chance.' I'd given up my job, I'd canceled California. I couldn't go back to Korea, not like that.

"At that time," Chung said, looking prosperous now in his La-Coste shirt and pleated chino pants, "I was maybe a little crazy."

Hard Beginnings

But he was also determined. On his first day of work, Chung learned that the workday of a greengrocer starts with choosing the merchandise and hauling the merchandise—three hours after midnight. By 7 A.M., he and his wife were opening their doors in a neighborhood where Spanish was as likely to be spoken as English.

Sun Y Chon had never worked a cash register, and neither she nor her husband knew how to use a scale. Sun's English was nonexistent. To explain a price, she would point to the figure on the cash register. In rapid-fire English and Spanish, impatient customers demanded fruits and vegetables the couple had never heard of in either language.

"One month later, I could not move my fingers," Chung said. "I could not pick up my pants and put them on. I never worked so hard in my life."

Exhausted each night after they closed, the pair retreated to their apartment, the awful fifth-floor walkup with the mice. They fed the children, enrolled by now in a nearby parochial school, put them to bed and contemplated the feeble family finances.

"During the day, we worked so hard we don't know how much money we were making, how much we were losing," Chung said. "We just kept running the store."

For three years, they worked that pace, day in, day out.

"Never a day off. Only Sundays, we went to church. That was it," Chung said. "No movies, no restaurants. We were just too tired to do anything."

Chung vowed he would make some changes the minute things turned around.

"As soon as I made some money, I was going to move to California," he said. "California had to be a better life."

Changing Fortunes

But Chung's fortunes did begin to change. The family amassed savings of nearly $40,000. Chung began looking for a house, and finally bought a $130,000 place in New Jersey, about 15 miles from the George Washington Bridge. For Christmas that year, 1979, he gave his wife a key to the still-unfinished house.

"All my friends in the church, they were very surprised because I was making money so fast," Chung said. "They knew that store. Three or four owners before me, nobody had made any money in that store." He smiled. "Maybe they did not work so hard."

"Every time they see me," Chung said of his acquaintances from their Korean-speaking Catholic church in Queens, "They call me the Hard Work Man."

Eventually Chung sold the Brooklyn store for $15,000 more than he had paid for it and bought a larger one in the Bronx. Then he began to set his eye on his current property, the California Fruit Market, in a Manhattan neighborhood composed largely of older Jewish residents and younger Spanish-speaking people.

Three years ago, Chung sold the Bronx store to concentrate his time and energy on the market in Manhattan. He does not like to talk about how much money he actually makes, and insists that high rent, salaries for his six employees and other expenses gobble up the profits. Even the 35% markup he charges over wholesale price barely covers his costs, he says.

"Right now, we save no money," he said. "You're lucky to break even now."

Eugene Kang, of the Korean Produce Assn., agrees that hefty profits are not necessarily a byproduct of the business. "I don't think it is so profitable," Kang said. "Believe me, it is not easy. They work very, very hard."

"That is the main thing," Chung concurred. "You've got to work so many hours. All the Korean grocers here, they all work 15-, 16-, 17-hour days, with their families. But employees, they don't want to work that hard that long."

Chung even advised his own brothers not to follow his path and move to America. "I tell them they have to work too hard," he said.

For Chung the day is a constant barrage of questions. "Where are the rutabagas?" "How much are the leeks?" "Do you have cilantro?" "Where's the fresh basil?" There are boxes to be filled, displays to be arranged, bruised produce to be disposed of.

Some customers haggle over prices. Others plead for free food. From a steady client, Chung will trade a ripe plum for the promise of a quarter.

Now Chung converses comfortably in Spanish, speaking easily to customers and his four Latino employees alike. Working the cash register, Sun Y Chon is less uncomfortable speaking English now.

The Next Generation

When they are in town, all three Chung children will sometimes work in the family store. Christine, 19, is studying international business at the University of Chicago. Clara, 24, has just finished nursing school. At 22, Augustine (also known by his Korean name, Jinsoo, or by his American nickname, Jake), is majoring in business at a small college on Staten Island, and studying for his real estate license.

■■■■■■■■■■■■■■■■■■■■■■■■■■■■■■■■■■■■

Chung jokes that his children speak Korean with a Bronx accent. Last summer, he sent them all to their home country for a long visit, their first since they left 13 years ago. They found it interesting, Chung said, but showed no interest in remaining.

"I'm just more comfortable here," said Jake, a strapping youth with gel-treated hair and hopes of becoming a New York real estate tycoon. "This is home."

Chung, lord of his small urban empire of mangoes and melons, grapefruits and green beans, would be hard pressed to disagree. America has been good to him, he said, and the American dream is real and can come true.

"Right now I am happy here," Chung said. "I've had no trouble until—" abruptly he brightened, "until last month when I got one speeding ticket."

Chung laughed hard. All those years of endless toil, mice on pillowcases, fingers that went on strike. All those trips to the Bronx produce warehouse in the middle of the night. All the confusion, the strange fruits, learning to count in Spanish. All that, and his one complaint is a speeding ticket?

There was a big smile on Chung's face as he calmly helped himself to a strawberry. He had earned it, after all.

■ ■ ■

••

Marie G. Lee

Marie G. Lee was born on April 25, 1964, in a town very much like Iron River, Minnesota, the setting for *Necessary Roughness*. Most of the residents of Hibbing, Minnesota, where Lee was born and raised, are Scandinavian. They originally came from the northern European countries of Sweden, Denmark, Norway, and Finland and generally have blond hair and blue eyes. Thus, the visual difference between them and people from minority groups is even more noticeable. Like Chan and Young in *Necessary Roughness,* Lee was the only Asian student—the only minority, in fact—in her high school. Although she was subject to some racial harassment, overall Lee felt like any typical American high school student. Her parents had come to the United States from Korea in 1953, but she had only ever lived in the United States. Like most American teenagers, she just wanted to fit in.

Lee was an accomplished writer even as a teenager. Her first essay was published in *Seventeen* magazine when she was sixteen years old. Early in her adolescence, Lee had little sense of her Korean roots. But slowly she began to realize that she was not the blond-haired, blue-eyed All-American girl featured in so many advertisements, magazines, and stories, and she became aware of her sometimes awkward position between two cultures: the Korea of her ancestors and the United States of her own experience. Her first novel, *Finding My Voice,* deals with the issue of being part of two ethnically diverse worlds.

A graduate of Brown University in Rhode Island, Lee now lectures at Yale University. In 2001, she lived and worked in Korea on a Fulbright Scholarship, a prestigious academic award. She has published six young adult novels, but has also written essays and stories for adults that have appeared in notable publications like *The New York Times.* Although Lee hopes her stories touch the lives of non-Asian, as well as Asian, readers, she admits that her efforts as a writer and her "perceptions of American life are inevitably filtered through a prism of race." It is not surprising, then, that she is also one of the founders of the Asian American Writers' Workshop. Based in New York City, the Workshop is a nonprofit organization created to provide support and resources for Asian writers living in the United States and for readers interested in their work.

■ ■ ■